NATIONAL GEOGRAPHIC

ANGRY BIRDS

A hungry
gull attacks
an innocent
bystander.

NATIONAL GEOGRAPHIC

ANGRY BIRDS

50 True Stories of the Fed Up, Feathered, and Furious

MEL WHITE ★ FOREWORD BY PETER VESTERBACKA

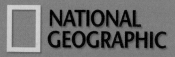

NATIONAL
GEOGRAPHIC

Washington, D.C.

Published by the National Geographic Society, 1145 17th Street N.W., Washington, D.C. 20036

Library of Congress Cataloging-in-Publication Data
White, Mel.
 National Geographic angry birds : 50 true stories of the fed up, feathered, and furious / Mel White ; foreword by
Peter Vesterbacka.
     p. cm.
 ISBN 978-1-4262-0996-3 (pbk.)
 1. Birds--Humor. 2. Bird watching--Humor. I. Title.
 PN6231.B46W48 2012
 818'.5407--dc23

                        2012012953

The National Geographic Society is one of the world's largest nonprofit scientific and educational organizations. Founded in 1888 to "increase and diffuse geographic knowledge," the Society's mission is to inspire people to care about the planet. It reaches more than 400 million people worldwide each month through its official journal, *National Geographic,* and other magazines; National Geographic Channel; television documentaries; music; radio; films; books; DVDs; maps; exhibitions; live events; school publishing programs; interactive media; and merchandise. National Geographic has funded more than 9,600 scientific research, conservation and exploration projects and supports an education program promoting geographic literacy.

For more information, visit **www.nationalgeographic.com.**
National Geographic Society
1145 17th Street N.W.
Washington, D.C. 20036-4688 U.S.A.

For information about special discounts for bulk purchases, please contact
National Geographic Books Special Sales: **ngspecsales@ngs.org**

For rights or permissions inquiries, please contact National Geographic Books
Subsidiary Rights. **ngbookrights@ngs.org**

Front cover image: Art Wolfe/www.artwolfe.com. Back cover image: Raymond Barlow/National Geographic My Shot.
Book design by Jonathan Halling and Stewart Bean
Printed in USA
12/WOR/2

Contents

Foreword: Fed Up, Feathered, and Furious 6

LEVEL 1 ANNOYED 8

LEVEL 2 TESTY 48

LEVEL 3 OUTRAGED 84

LEVEL 4 FURIOUS 120

featuring The World's Angriest Bird

Angry Birds in Scientific Order 156
Acknowledgments 158
Illustration Credits 159

Fed Up, Feathered, and Furious

Since we first released Angry Birds, we've gotten all kinds of fan art from cakes to sandcastles to jewelry and everything in between! But one consistent fan favorite has always been pictures of Angry Birds "in the wild"—realistic-looking birds with peeved expressions and thick black eyebrows.

So what does a real-life Angry Bird look like?

National Geographic has taken on the challenge and found some of nature's most furious birds. From a bit grumpy to downright livid, these birds are angry and they're not going to take it anymore! And really, can you blame them? When their nest is threatened or someone trespasses on their territory, they have to take action.

But as the birds in this book demonstrate, a little bit of anger goes a long way. Geese terrorizing college students and pelicans attacking cameras look more ridiculous than righteous.

So as you read more about the original Angry Birds and their real-life counterparts, we hope you'll get a good laugh out of these furious fowl. Just remember to save your own anger for the annoying green piggies!

Peter Vesterbacka
Mighty Eagle & CMO
Rovio Entertainment Ltd.

LEVEL 1 ANNOYED

(adj.) harassed, especially by quick, brief attacks

A Hawfinch, right, quarrels with a Eurasian Tree Sparrow.

RAP SHEET

NAME: THE BLUES

PHYSICAL DESCRIPTION: SMALL, ROUND, BLUE BIRDS

ALIAS: THE BLUES

HOW ANGRY ARE THEY: ANNOYED

WHAT MAKES THEM ANGRY: BEING SCOLDED AND BEING IGNORED. PIGS.

ANGRY BEHAVIORS: SPECIALIZING IN GROUP ATTACKS, BUT ALSO SEEN ATTACKING AS ONE. STRONG AFFINITY FOR BREAKING ICE

HOBBIES: MUSIC, ACTING, DRAWING

STRONGEST ALLY: EACH OTHER

THREE'S COMPANY, TOO:
THE BLUES

Out of all the Angry Birds, it is the happy-go-lucky Blues who understand the true power of teamwork. Never apart, the three birds play together, get mad together, and attack together.

THE BLUES' STORY

The youngest members of the Angry Birds bunch, the Blues are always looking for new adventures. Curiously playful and daring, they are very imaginative and masters of mimicry.

The adventurous Blues strive to be like their heroes, Red and Mighty Eagle, and they despise the pigs who steal their eggs. They regularly act out the great battles of the other birds. And it is while the Blues are concentrating on their games that they occasionally drift away from their guard duty and leave the eggs unprotected. It is often when the Blues are guarding the eggs that the pigs manage to snatch them.

WHAT MAKES THEM ANGRY

Babies of the bunch, the Blues occasionally get distracted while guarding the eggs. They don't like to be blamed for the eggs' being snatched (even if they are responsible!), so they try to cover up their oversight. The three birds are usually able to recapture the eggs before the rest of the bunch realize they have been taken.

Helmeted Guineafowl (*Numida meleagris*)

We should hire him to be our watch bird!

RAP SHEET

SPECIES: HELMETED GUINEAFOWL (*NUMIDA MELEAGRIS*)

PHYSICAL DESCRIPTION: DARK PLUMP BODY SPECKLED WITH WHITE, 24 IN (61 CM) LONG, 2.8 LB (1.3 KG); BONY GROWTH ("HELMET") ON HEAD

KNOWN WHEREABOUTS: SOUTHERN AFRICA

ALIASES: GUINEAHEN

ANGRY BEHAVIORS: LOUD, RAUCOUS, AND STRIDENT ALARM CALLS WHEN DANGER APPROACHES

JUNKYARD GUINEAFOWL

In their native southern Africa, Helmeted Guineafowl make tasty snacks for predators from leopards to jackals to eagles. Because they hang around in flocks, these chicken-like birds have evolved loud, angry cries to warn others about the presence of danger. And because we humans are sometimes fairly clever, we've found a way to use that instinct for our own benefit.

BEWARE OF GUINEAFOWL

African villagers have long kept guineafowl around their houses to warn of lions and other dangerous animals. When the species was brought to Europe from Africa for food, rural Europeans soon learned that the birds could also serve as feathered watchdogs. Farmers found that guineafowl would squawk loudly when a fox or hawk came hunting for a meal, giving the chickens, ducks, geese, and other barnyard animals a chance to run for cover.

By now, guineafowl have spread around the world. They breed prolifically and need less upkeep and prepared food than other poultry, and their popularity on the dinner table has had a recent resurgence. Yet many people keep them mainly for their role as sentries, counting on the odd-looking fowl to sound an alarm not only about wild predators but about human trespassers as well.

And it's not only rural folk who utilize the watchfulness of guineafowl. One car dealership in London installed a small flock of guineafowl as security guards—effective and willing to work for far less than minimum wage.

NEED MORE SUGAR!

RAP SHEET

SPECIES: RUFOUS HUMMINGBIRD (*SELASPHORUS RUFUS*)

PHYSICAL DESCRIPTION: RUFOUS PLUMAGE WITH GREENISH TINGE, 3.75 IN (10 CM) LONG, 0.15 OZ (4.2 G)

KNOWN WHEREABOUTS: NESTS IN NORTHWESTERN NORTH AMERICA; WINTERS MOSTLY IN MEXICO

ALIASES: HUMMER; MIGHT BE MISTAKEN FOR ALLEN'S HUMMINGBIRD

ANGRY BEHAVIORS: DIVE-BOMBS RIVALS, FLASHING SHINY THROAT AND FLARING TAIL

Pair of Rufous Hummingbirds

THEY AIN'T SWEET

Parents warning their children about the dangers of too much sugar should use the hummingbird as an example of what can go wrong: hyperactivity, irritability, aggression—all the classic symptoms of a kid on a sugar high. Though this bird gets its rush from flower nectar, not candy bars and soft drinks.

TINY TERROR

Ounce for ounce, hummingbirds probably top the list of aggressive birds. The Rufous Hummingbird of western North America might be the angriest hummer of all—possibly because it migrates farther in relation to its body size than any other bird and needs every bit of nourishment it can get. When this mite finds a flower patch it perches nearby and angrily zooms in to chase off any bird looking to share.

There's a reason for this selfish bullying, though, and it boils down to a simple fact: A hummingbird has to eat almost constantly or it will die. No other animal has a metabolism as high as a hovering hummingbird. And since food enters and exits a hummingbird's body in less than an hour, it has to eat almost constantly. If a hummer maintained its regular metabolism it would starve to death overnight. To prevent this, hummers go into a low-energy state called "torpor," during which their breathing rate, heartbeat, and temperature drop, cutting their energy need more than 90 percent.

The notoriously aggressive Rufous Hummingbird prepares for the long ordeal of migration with an orgy of eating, increasing its body fat by nearly three-quarters. Fat and happy? Fat and angry is more like it.

Adélie Penguin (Pygoscelis adeliae)

KEEP YOUR STINKIN' BEAKS OFF MY ROCKS!

LEVEL 1 ANNOYED

RAP SHEET

SPECIES: ADÉLIE PENGUIN (PYGOSCELIS ADELIAE)

PHYSICAL DESCRIPTION: BLACK-AND-WHITE FLIGHTLESS BIRD, 28 IN (71 CM) TALL, 12 LB (5.4 KG)

KNOWN WHEREABOUTS: ANTARCTICA

ALIASES: MIGHT BE MISTAKEN FOR CHINSTRAP PENGUIN OR GENTOO PENGUIN

ANGRY BEHAVIORS: STEALS NEST ROCKS; LUNGING AND PECKING

NO STONE LEFT UNTURNED

Adélie Penguins have a tough life. They live in Antarctica, one of Earth's angriest environments. Eighty percent don't survive to their first birthday. Nesting adults may have to make a round trip of 150 miles or more just to find something to eat. Whenever they go for a swim, hungry leopard seals are waiting to snack on them. And on top of all that, they have to put up with criminals sabotaging their love lives.

ROCK YOUR WORLD

In breeding season, male Adélies arrive first at colonies, immediately beginning to build "nests": circular piles of rocks a few inches high. Females show up later, many looking for new sweethearts.

CAUGHT IN THE ACT

One of the ways females judge males is by the quality of their nests. Some males waddle long distances to find just the right mix of stones and pebbles. Others take a more devious route: When the conscientious builder isn't looking, they sneak in to steal rocks from his nest **(see "Caught in the Act").**

Of course, sometimes these penguin thieves get caught, and what follows is an angry confrontation with much wing-flapping, squawking, and pecking.

Adélie colonies contain thousands of birds packed tightly together, so the stone burglars and their victims create lots of loud, aggressive interaction. It's a shame the hard-working penguins have to put up with criminals in their midst, but all's fair in love and war—even a battle for rocks.

House Wren
(*Troglodytes aedon*)

AAAAAARGH!

RAP SHEET

SPECIES: HOUSE WREN (*TROGLODYTES AEDON*)

PHYSICAL DESCRIPTION: VERY SMALL BROWNISH BIRD, ABOUT 5 IN (12 CM) LONG, 0.4 OZ (11 G)

KNOWN WHEREABOUTS: FROM ALASKA TO SOUTHERN SOUTH AMERICA; OFTEN NESTS AROUND SUBURBAN YARDS AND BUILDINGS, ESPECIALLY IN BIRDHOUSES

ALIASES: JENNY WREN; EASILY MISTAKEN FOR THE SMALLER WINTER WREN

ANGRY BEHAVIORS: NOISY ALARM REACTION, "MOBBING" PREDATORS; HIGHLY AGGRESSIVE TO OTHER SMALL BIRDS

THE LEADER OF THE PACK

You know the feisty little guy who somehow ends up in the middle of all the action? Think about Jimmy Cagney in those old gangster movies: He wasn't the biggest guy in the room, but his personality always made him the gang leader. That's the House Wren.

Individually, small birds don't have much of a chance against a marauding cat, hawk, owl, or even pig. Their best hope is an activity known as "mobbing," in which lots of birds crowd the predator, make noise, dart around distractingly, and collectively try to convince it to get lost. Once the element of surprise is gone, the intruder usually retreats to try again somewhere else.

DO NOT DISTURB

Smaller than a sparrow, the wren is often the first bird on the block to raise the alarm when danger is near and acts as the de facto mob leader. Few birds are more easily irritated, and ounce for ounce, none are louder. One early naturalist wrote, "When disturbed, and it takes little to disturb a house wren, the bird bursts forth with a sharp, tense chatter"—a sound called "scolding" that instantly alerts and attracts other species.

That's not the only angry aspect of the House Wren, either. It's highly aggressive toward bird neighbors, especially if they're competitors for nest sites. House Wrens are known to enter other birds' nests, puncture eggs, and kill nestlings. In the old days, when moralistic nature-lovers felt compelled to classify birds as either "good" or "bad," House Wrens were definitely on the naughty list. Today we know better than to make such anthropomorphic judgments—but the House Wren's angry acts serve it well as the leader of the mob.

A female Common Kingfisher behaves aggressively with her male counterpart.

LEVEL 1 ANNOYED

When vying for fishing spots, kingfishers may lock beaks and try to wrestle each other underwater.

21

RAP SHEET

SPECIES: GREAT WHITE PELICAN (*PELECANUS ONOCROTALUS*)

PHYSICAL DESCRIPTION: VERY LARGE WHITE-AND-BLACK BIRD, UP TO 5 FT (1.6 M) LONG WITH WINGSPAN TO 8 FT (2.6 M), 18 LB (8.2 KG)

KNOWN WHEREABOUTS: SOUTH CENTRAL EURASIA, SOUTH ASIA AND AFRICA

ALIASES: MIGHT BE MISTAKEN FOR AUSTRALIAN PELICAN OR SPOT-BILLED PELICAN

ANGRY BEHAVIORS: LUNGES WITH LARGE BILL WHEN IT FEELS CORNERED OR THREATENED

A Great White Pelican interrupts a man trying to read his newspaper.

NOBODY PUTS PELICAN IN THE CORNER

If there's a bird equivalent of the Hollywood star who loves bright lights and red carpets, we can assume it's definitely not the pelican. There must be something about show biz that brings out the grumpy side of this normally chilled-out animal.

HALIBUT, NOT HOLLYWOOD

Pelicans have attacked people appearing with them on live television for no apparent reason—unless it was sheer camera-shyness. An Australian weatherman broadcasting from the Sydney Zoo felt a pelican's wrath as the big bird lunged at him, driving him into a corner and pecking him repeatedly with its strong, sharp bill (see "Caught in the Act"). Another time, a bird expert brought a pelican with him to a St. Louis television station, and just as he was starting his presentation, the animal guest struck him twice in the groin, causing the man to double over in pain.

CAUGHT IN THE ACT

Often a pelican "attack" has nothing to do with bad temper. In waterfront areas pelicans sometimes get accustomed to being fed and approach people assuming they're carrying food. If something shiny—a camera or phone—looks to the pelican like a fish, it may make a grab for the "meal."

Other times, people simply get too close while trying for the perfect photo. When the pelican lunges toward the shutterbug, it's just saying, "Hey, give me some room here, buddy!"

||||||||||||||||||||||||||||||||||||||||||||||||||||||||||||||||||||||||||||||||||||||||||||||||||||||||||||

Yellow Warbler (*Setophaga petechia*)

RAP SHEET

SPECIES: YELLOW WARBLER (*SETOPHAGA PETECHIA*)

PHYSICAL DESCRIPTION: SMALL BRIGHT-YELLOW SONGBIRD, 5 IN (13 CM) LONG, 0.35 OZ (10 G)

KNOWN WHEREABOUTS: ALASKA TO NORTHERN SOUTH AMERICA

ALIASES: GOLDEN WARBLER, MANGROVE WARBLER

ANGRY BEHAVIORS: SEALS UP COWBIRD EGGS TO PREVENT THEM FROM HATCHING

DON'T GET MAD, GET EVEN

It sounds like the plot of a Hollywood thriller: Parents come home to find their child missing, while an intruder has substituted one of her own. Yet it happens all the time for birds living near cowbirds.

These members of the blackbird family are brood parasites, which means they make no nest of their own. Instead, female cowbirds furtively lay eggs in other birds' nests, expecting the foster parents to raise the young cowbirds (see "Caught in the Act").

CAUGHT IN THE ACT

PARASITES BEWARE

Many birds fall for the scheme, not recognizing the strange egg and raising the cowbird young as their own. Of the birds that spot the odd egg, some throw it out, while others abandon the nest and start over. But the Yellow Warbler has a special approach: It raises the walls of its nest and builds a new floor over the cowbird egg (and sometimes one or more of its own eggs). This may happen several times. One warbler nest was found to have six stories, the bottom five sealing up cowbird eggs.

It's like the bird version of Edgar Allan Poe's macabre story "The Cask of Amontillado": Someone who's been wronged gets vengeance by sealing up the evildoer in a tomb—while the hapless victim is still living. You could call the Yellow Warbler an architect of revenge.

‖‖

RAP SHEET

SPECIES: EURASIAN MAGPIE (*PICA PICA*)

PHYSICAL DESCRIPTION: MEDIUM-SIZE BODY WITH VERY LONG TAIL, TOGETHER TOTALING 19 IN (48 CM), 6 OZ (175 G); STRIKING BLACK-AND-WHITE PLUMAGE WITH DARK FEATHERS SHOWING BLUE-GREEN IRIDESCENCE

KNOWN WHEREABOUTS: MOST OF EUROPE AND ASIA

ALIASES: MAGGOT-PIE; EASILY MISTAKEN FOR BLACK-BILLED MAGPIE

ANGRY BEHAVIORS: CURIOUS, BOLD, AND AT LEAST SOMETIMES KLEPTOMANIACAL

I like shiny things, too!

Eurasian Magpie
(*Pica pica*)

THE NOTORIOUS MAG P.I.E.

The wise owl, the sly fox, the brave lion—all these animals gained their near-mythical status because of what humans saw as admirable qualities. But the magpie became a legend for larceny. After all, how many birds are such reprobates they've had an opera written about their misdeeds?

JEWELS AND JOKERS

The magpie can't help its criminal instincts. Evolution has given this bird an addiction to shiny things, and it's not above stealing whatever catches its eye. Usually the behavior is only annoying—for instance, one magpie in England became notorious for flying into a mechanic's shop to snatch tools and car keys. But in Rossini's famous opera *La Gazza Ladra (The Thieving Magpie),* the bad bird almost causes a real tragedy. A poor servant girl is condemned to death when her mistress accuses her of stealing a silver spoon. (Justice was harsh in those days.) The culprit, of course, is a passing magpie. When the feathered criminal is seen stealing a coin, the spoon is found in its nest. The innocent girl goes free, and everybody lives happily ever after.

Lewis and Clark were the first explorers to see the American magpie. While they were at Fort Mandan (in present-day North Dakota) in 1805, they sent four live magpies to Thomas Jefferson, who noted with surprise that the bird looked like the ones he'd seen in France. In Lewis and Clark's journals, they describe how magpies entered tents to steal food right off tables.

Magpies belong to the crow family, a group often considered to be the world's smartest birds. So not only do they have the desire to steal, they've got the brains to pull off their heists.

A Fieldfare (right) fights with a male blackbird over apples in the snow.

RAP SHEET

SPECIES: FIELDFARE
(*TURDUS PILARIS*)

PHYSICAL DESCRIPTION: MEDIUM-SIZE SONGBIRD WITH BLUE-GRAY BACK AND REDDISH CHEST, 10 IN (25 CM), 3.5 OZ (100 G)

KNOWN WHEREABOUTS: MUCH OF EUROPE AND ASIA

ALIASES: BLUETAIL, STORM BIRD

ANGRY BEHAVIORS: SPRAYS DROPPINGS ON BIRD PREDATORS

FIELDFARE SAYS
BOMBS AWAY!

Even normally placid birds can turn into flying tigers when their eggs or young are threatened. Defense of the nest typically involves swooping at an intruder, squawking loudly, and sometimes threats of (or real) pecking. But the Fieldfare, a European thrush, has perfected a team strategy as effective as it is nasty.

DEADLY DOO-DOO

Thrushes usually nest individually, but Fieldfares often breed in colonies of up to 40 pairs. When a known predator such as a raven appears, the Fieldfares give a raspy alarm call that gathers defenders from all over the colony. Not only do these thrushes swoop at the predator, they also eject droppings as they dive, timing their bombing precisely to splatter the enemy with their smelly poop. Although a raven is much larger and more powerful than a Fieldfare, it quickly retreats, leaving the eggs and helpless nestlings unharmed.

Ick, nasty—right? But the attack is more than just unpleasant. The droppings saturate the predator's feathers, destroying their vital insulating ability. If there's rain or a temperature drop, the attacker could actually die from the Fieldfares' putrid ploy.

Fieldfares learned that their splattering strategy doesn't work for stoats (weasels), because mammal fur isn't affected the way feathers are. When a stoat appears, Fieldfares keep quiet, hoping they'll be undetected. In areas with lots of stoats, Fieldfares often breed singly rather than in colonies, making it harder for their mammalian enemy to find nests.

RAP SHEET

NAME: MATILDA

PHYSICAL DESCRIPTION: WHITE EGG-SHAPED BIRD

ALIAS: WHITE BIRD

HOW ANGRY IS SHE: ANNOYED

WHAT MAKES HER ANGRY: DAMAGING OR DEFILING NATURE. PIGS.

ANGRY BEHAVIORS: VERTICALLY EGGING PIGGY FORTRESSES AND PIGS

HOBBIES: GARDENING, BIOLOGY

STRONGEST ALLY: BOMB

GIVE PEACE A CHANCE: MATILDA

Most of the time, Matilda isn't angry. In fact, she strives to be peaceful. But it's not always easy being the peace lover amid a roost of Angry Birds and a kleptomaniacal drove of pigs. Matilda is not easily angered herself, and often tries to find a calmer way to solve the Angry Birds' problems.

MATILDA'S STORY

Matilda loves nature and anything with a good aura. To quiet her mind and commune with nature she often goes for long nature walks and collects stones, pebbles, and other pretty things that catch her eye. She uses these trinkets to create a necklace, one that she hopes symbolizes a future peace for her and the Angry Birds. She looks to the natural world for signs of a peaceful future for the birds and the pigs.

Matilda believes in a healthy lifestyle, and tries to pass that on to the rest of the birds. They politely put up with her health drinks and health food concoctions despite their questionable flavor. But Bomb (aka Black Bird), desperate to work on his explosive temper, turns to Matilda's herbal teas and liniments.

WHAT MAKES HER ANGRY

Pollution, waste, and exploitation infuriate the otherwise peace-loving Matilda. Even though she dreams of a world where pigs and birds can live in harmony, she finds the pigs' shameless exploitation of wildlife and waste of natural resources most infuriating. When enraged she sabotages the pigs' structures and fortresses by bombarding them with her own (potentially explosive) eggs.

RAP SHEET

SPECIES: TOCO TOUCAN
(*RAMPHASTOS TOCO*)

PHYSICAL DESCRIPTION: BLACK
BODY, WHITE NECK, AND MASSIVE
ORANGE BILL; 24 IN (61 CM) LONG,
30 OZ (850 G)

KNOWN WHEREABOUTS:
EASTERN SOUTH AMERICA

ALIASES: KEEL-BILLED TOUCAN
IS KNOWN AS "BILL BIRD"; TOUCAN
SAM IS THE FROOT LOOPS BIRD

ANGRY BEHAVIORS: USES MASSIVE
BILL TO NAB EGGS AND NESTLINGS

This guy's
as bad as
a pig!

Toco Toucan
(*Ramphastos toco*)

MY, WHAT A BIG BILL YOU HAVE!

What bird can conjure up more fun than a toucan can? One look at this goofy creature, with its clownishly outsized bill, and you're instantly in a good mood. Advertisers know this: Toucans have been used to sell everything from beer to children's cereal to tropical resorts. The Central American country of Belize chose the Keel-billed Toucan as its national bird, representing its colorful rain forest wildlife to potential vacationers. But there's another side to the toucan, too. While its amazing bill is used mostly to pluck fruit from hard-to-get-to tree branches, it's also put to a very different use when the toucan turns predator.

ALL THE BETTER TO EAT YOU WITH

South America's Toco Toucan of has the largest bill in relation to its body of any bird. When it gets hungry for baby birds or eggs, it uses its long bill to reach into nest cavities to satisfy its urge for a snack. The size and bright color of the bill can intimidate parents into fleeing, and the massive beak can be used as a weapon against any bird that puts up a fight. Smaller birds that are often victimized by toucans recognize them as enemies, screaming warnings when toucans approach and flying out to harass them just as if they were hawks. Birds called oropendolas often purposely breed near nests of bees or wasps, which helps protect them from hungry toucans.

For a bird-watcher, it's always a thrill to see a gaudily beautiful toucan sitting in a rain forest tree. But for a small bird with a nest nearby, it's no fun at all.

RAP SHEET

SPECIES: NORTHERN CARDINAL (*CARDINALIS CARDINALIS*)

PHYSICAL DESCRIPTION: MEDIUM-SIZE SONGBIRD, 8.5 IN (22 CM) LONG, 1.6 OZ (45 G); MALES RED, FEMALES REDDISH-BROWN

KNOWN WHEREABOUTS: EASTERN UNITED STATES AND MOST OF MEXICO

ALIASES: REDBIRD, CARDINAL GROSBEAK

ANGRY BEHAVIORS: ATTACKS ITS OWN IMAGE IN MIRRORS

YOU TALKIN' TO ME? YOU TALKIN' TO ME?

A male Northern Cardinal attacks its own reflection.

PUT 'EM UP, PUT 'EM UP

Birds occasionally do things that remind us of an inescapable truth: They're beautiful and they have amazing skills, but sometimes they're not too smart. Such is the answer to the question, "Why is that bird attacking its reflection?"

Several species do this, but the most notorious is the Northern Cardinal. Both males and females fight their own images, and the basic reason is rooted in the desire to raise young successfully. Once a pair has established a nesting territory, they defend it against other intruding cardinals—males try to drive away males, and females chase females. Evolution has proved that's a good way to make sure they'll be able to find enough food for their nestlings.

MIRROR, MIRROR ON THE WALL

Unfortunately, evolution has not taught them that their reflection in a window, a patio door, or a car's rearview mirror isn't a different bird. A cardinal is programmed to attack a bird that looks like itself until the rival flees, and nothing looks more like itself than a reflection—but this rival won't go away.

If a cardinal, or any other bird, repeatedly attacks a reflection, the cure is simply to remove the reflecting surface. Tape a newspaper page to the window or cover the car's side mirror with a cloth. The bird's urge lasts only through nesting season.
Once its hormones subside, so will its need to fight rivals.

It's true: Birds lack our reasoning ability. On the other hand, wouldn't it be nice to be able to fly?

35

Crested
Bellbird
(*Oreoica
gutturalis*)

THE BEST
OFFENSE IS
A GOOD
DEFENSE.

RAP SHEET

SPECIES: CRESTED BELLBIRD
(*OREOICA GUTTURALIS*)

PHYSICAL DESCRIPTION: GRAY-
BROWN WITH BLACK CHEST BAND,
9 IN (22 CM) LONG, 2.3 OZ (65 G)

KNOWN WHEREABOUTS: AUSTRALIA

ALIASES: DICK-DICK-THE-DEVIL
(IMITATING ITS CALL)

ANGRY BEHAVIORS: PARALYZES
POISONOUS CATERPILLARS TO
PROTECT NEST

NEST OF THE LIVING DEAD

How do you survive if you're a small, defenseless songbird in the Australian Outback, where all sorts of predators are waiting to invade your nest and eat your eggs or nestlings?

The Crested Bellbird has developed a bizarre strategy to protect its home, even when the parent birds aren't around. It creates an army of poisonous zombies—a mass of living-dead insects forming a defensive perimeter circling the nest.

KILLER CATERPILLARS

As soon as the adult bellbirds have constructed their nest, they search the countryside nearby for certain types of hairy caterpillars. These moth larvae have thousands of hairs on their bodies, tiny hollow spines capable of stinging and injecting poison into whatever touches them. In humans, the poison can cause itching, swelling, and sometimes severe pain. For a few highly allergic people, touching a stinging caterpillar can even cause death.

The parent bellbird brings the caterpillars home and places them around the edge of the nest. Why don't the caterpillars simply crawl away? Because the bellbird knows just how to pinch the caterpillar bodies with its bill, leaving them alive but paralyzed. Before long, the rim of the bellbird nest is a mass of writhing, hairy bugs, ready to sting any rat or quoll (a carnivorous marsupial) that comes looking for a meal of baby bellbirds.

In another odd adaptation, newly hatched bellbirds have long, hairlike feathers on their bodies, which gives them an appearance similar to hairy caterpillars. The sight reinforces the warning to potential predators: Stay away!

Jaegers often lurk around penguin breeding grounds to try to swipe their eggs.

LEVEL 1 ANNOYED

38

Two Gentoo
Penguins ward off
a Parasitic Jaeger.

Magnificent
Frigatebirds
take flight
at sunset.

A HIGH-FLYING LIFE of CRIME

Scientists have a fancy name for it—kleptoparasitism—but most people would just call it stealing. Whatever you call its shady behavior, the Magnificent Frigatebird proves that sometimes crime does pay.

DANGER IN THE HIGH-SKIES

This tropical seabird has a reputation as the pirate of the bird world, using its astonishing flying skill to chase and harass other birds to force them to give up food they're carrying. This isn't just simple pickpocketing, either; it's aggravated assault. The frigatebird often grabs victims with its long, hooked bill and sometimes even flips them upside-down. When a weaker bird drops its food, the frigatebird zooms down and catches the ill-gained booty in midair. Its most common victims include pelicans, cormorants, gulls, and terns, as well as other frigatebirds. The frigatebird isn't a total moocher, though. It also swoops low over the sea to scoop up small fish, squid, and even young sea turtles.

The name "frigatebird" came from this species' resemblance to a type of fast, graceful sailing ship, but the folk name Man-o'-War Bird relates directly to its fearsome piracy. And "magnificent"? Well, no matter how much of a rogue the frigatebird is, you can't help admiring the beauty of its form and function.

No other bird in the world has such large wings—they're more than eight feet (2.4 meters) from tip to tip—in relation to its weight: only about four pounds (1.9 kilograms).

Continued on p. 42

This wing-to-weight ratio ("wing-loading," as it's called by aeronautical engineers) gives the frigatebird unmatched maneuverability. It's hard for a frigatebird to take off from flat ground or water, which is why it almost always perches on something elevated, such as a tree limb or ship's mast. Once it takes off, though, it can soar seemingly forever without flapping its wings, taking advantage of the rising air in thermal currents just as gliders do. For potential victims, the frigatebird's wings might as well be the Jolly Roger flapping in the wind.

Oddly enough, the frigatebird looks its angriest not when it's bullying other birds but when it's courting. Males have a patch of bright-red bare skin on their throat, similar to the pouch of pelicans. When a male frigatebird wants to attract a female, he inflates his throat sac to enormous size, so it seems as if he has a scarlet balloon around his neck. It looks painful and maybe even frightening, but the female frigatebird finds it irresistible. A whole colony of displaying male frigatebirds resembles a vast, low-lying Christmas tree.

RAP SHEET

SPECIES: MAGNIFICENT FRIGATEBIRD (FREGATA MAGNIFICENS)

PHYSICAL DESCRIPTION: LARGE BLACK BIRD WITH LONG FORKED TAIL AND SLENDER WINGS MORE THAN 8 FT (2.4 M) ACROSS, 3.9 LB (1.8 KG); FEMALES AND IMMATURE BIRDS HAVE VARYING AMOUNTS OF WHITE ON BODY

KNOWN WHEREABOUTS: TROPICAL AND SUBTROPICAL SEAS IN THE ATLANTIC, CARIBBEAN, AND EASTERN PACIFIC

ALIASES: MAN-O'-WAR BIRD, HURRICANE BIRD

ANGRY BEHAVIORS: HARASSES AND STEALS FOOD FROM OTHER BIRDS

Two female
Magnificent
Frigatebirds
in flight

Tui (*Prosthemadera novaeseelandiae*)

GO BACK TO WHERE YOU CAME FROM!

RAP SHEET

SPECIES: TUI (*PROSTHEMADERA NOVAESEELANDIAE*)

PHYSICAL DESCRIPTION: MEDIUM-SIZE SONGBIRD WITH IRIDESCENT BLACK PLUMAGE, 11 IN (30 CM) LONG, 4.4 OZ (125 G)

KNOWN WHEREABOUTS: NEW ZEALAND

ALIASES: PARSON BIRD

ANGRY BEHAVIORS: ATTACKS WITH RAUCOUS CRIES AND VIGOROUS WING FLAPPING

WHEN ALIENS ATTACK

What do you do when aliens invade your country, wiping out entire communities and taking over vast tracts of land? If you're an angry bird, or Will Smith, you fight back.

EUROPEAN INVASION

When European settlers arrived in New Zealand, they brought with them all sorts of plants and animals not found naturally on the islands. The result was devastation of the ecosystem, as foxes, weasels, cats, and possums slaughtered native species that had evolved without defenses against land predators. Some birds have been driven to extinction, and many others barely hang onto existence.

The Tui, though, is aggressive enough to resist the invaders. It remains common over much of New Zealand, its wonderful variety of calls heard in forest and suburban gardens. (The Maori say of a skilled speaker that he "has the throat of a Tui.") While Tuis don't have weapons to fight weasels, their overall aggressiveness has helped them in the tough battle for survival. When alien mynah birds try to kill their nestlings, Tuis puff themselves up, shriek loudly, and dive and peck vigorously to drive away the would-be predators. In fact, Tuis aren't afraid to go after much larger hawks and falcons.

Tuis are known as great mimics, not only of natural sounds but of mechanical noises such as cell phones. Like parrots, they can be taught to imitate human speech. And how's this for smart? Tuis even mimic the alarm calls of other species to scare them away from feeding and nesting sites.

RAP SHEET

SPECIES: EASTERN KINGBIRD (*TYRANNUS TYRANNUS*)

PHYSICAL DESCRIPTION: SMALL SONGBIRD, BLACK AND DARK GRAY ABOVE, WHITE BELOW, WITH A WHITE BAND ACROSS THE TAIL TIP; ABOUT 8 IN (22 CM) LONG, 1.4 OZ (40 G)

KNOWN WHEREABOUTS: BREEDS ACROSS MUCH OF NORTH AMERICA AND WINTERS IN SOUTH AMERICA; NESTS IN TREES IN OPEN COUNTRY

ALIASES: BEE MARTIN; EASILY MISTAKEN FOR LOGGERHEAD KINGBIRD OR GIANT KINGBIRD

ANGRY BEHAVIORS: VERY HOSTILE TOWARD PREDATORS LARGER THAN ITSELF

An Eastern Kingbird mobs a Red-tailed Hawk.

THE BIRD WHO WOULD BE KING

How combative do you have to be to earn the title "Tyrant Tyrant"? The Eastern Kingbird's scientific name, *Tyrannus tyrannus,* is completely appropriate, because this little bird acts like it rules the world. Not much bigger than a sparrow, the kingbird not only won't back down from a fight, but goes out of its way to attack birds far larger than itself—and dominates by sheer aggressiveness.

I'm rooting for the little guy!

HOLDING COURT

Blue jays, crows, hawks—whipping them is child's play for a kingbird. A squirrel looking for a lunch of kingbird eggs faces the tyrant's fury and usually retreats. One naturalist reported a kingbird attacking a Great Egret (with a wingspan of more than four feet) over a distance of 100 yards, "practically riding on its back." Another astounding story has a kingbird chasing a low-flying airplane that passed near its nest.

King of the birds, indeed! The Eastern Kingbird has a bright scarlet crown that it keeps hidden unless something makes it angry—which happens often. When a kingbird gets mad, in the words of one writer, its flight becomes "a zigzag of blind rage." Two males meeting zoom together, lock claws, pull each other's feathers out, and crash to the ground before one gives up and flees.

When early European settlers in America watched the domineering antics of this species, they named it for the king it seemed to be. It just goes to prove that you don't have to be big to be powerful. Anybody ever hear of a guy named Napoleon?

LEVEL 2 ⟩ TESTY

(adj.) marked by impatience or ill humor

Common
buzzards in
a fighting
match

49

RAP SHEET

NAME: TERENCE

PHYSICAL DESCRIPTION: LARGE, ROUND, DARK RED BIRD

ALIAS: BIG BROTHER

HOW ANGRY IS HE: TESTY

WHAT MAKES HIM ANGRY: PIGS. AND PIGS.

ANGRY BEHAVIORS: PIG SQUASHING, SMASHING THROUGH EVERYTHING IN HIS PATH

HOBBIES: STARING CONTESTS

STRONGEST ALLY: RED

SILENT, BUT DEADLY:
TERENCE

Destruction is what the Angry Birds do best, but when it comes to complete and total annihilation, it's Terence who can deliver a crushing blow. Suddenly appearing out of nowhere, Terence is potentially the deadliest weapon the Angry Birds have.

TERENCE'S STORY

Terence has not spoken a word since his childhood, when he witnessed the cruelty of constant conflict with the pigs. Terence is deeply haunted by his past and can't shake the violent memories of his youth.

Because of his unpredictable violent streak, the other birds fear that Terence might damage the eggs. Therefore, Terence lives in self-imposed isolation in an abandoned piggy fortress, totally removed from the rest of the Angry Birds. Red understands that Terence is searching for his lost childhood and is the only one Terence is still able to connect with.

WHAT MAKES HIM ANGRY

Pigs enrage Terence. When Terence sees or thinks he sees one, he causes the most damage and destruction. All the emotion he keeps pent up inside literally explodes, and his increased size and mass allow him to destroy everything and anything in his path. Nothing can stop him. Terence doesn't enjoy being angry, but his deep-seated pig hatred makes it an inevitable, albeit unpleasant, part of life.

RAP SHEET

SPECIES: RUFF *(PHILOMACHUS PUGNAX)*

PHYSICAL DESCRIPTION: MALES MULTICOLORED IN SPRING, 13 IN (32 CM) LONG, 5.8 OZ (165 G); FEMALES SMALLER AND BROWNISH

KNOWN WHEREABOUTS: NORTHERN EUROPE AND ASIA

ALIASES: REE, REEVE (FEMALES ONLY)

ANGRY BEHAVIORS: MALES LUNGE AT AND PECK RIVALS

They're not worried about rufflin' any feathers.

A male Ruff displays courtship behavior with another Ruff.

SOME LIKE IT RUFF

An aggressive sandpiper? That doesn't seem right . . . Sandpipers are those shy, dull-gray birds that run around the beach, silently searching for something to eat in the sand, right?

In the case of the Ruff, wrong. This sandpiper flaunts some of the fanciest feathering of any species, and the males' spring courtship contests gave it the scientific name *Philomachus pugnax,* which means "pugnacious battle-lover." The Ruff acts angry, but while the battles are going on, the action behind the scenes is like something from a scandalous daytime soap opera.

DRESSED TO IMPRESS

In spring, Ruffs migrate north to their breeding grounds in northern Europe and Asia. Most males display long, puffy, multicolored feathers around the head and neck, with no two looking exactly the same. (The species' common name, of course, came from the elaborate neck decorations called ruffs that high-society people wore in Shakespeare's time.) Males gather at sites called "leks," where they pose, "dance," show off their plumage, and generally act like fashion models on the runway, all to attract females for mating. They also fight constantly, jabbing at and pecking one another to establish dominance, trying to mate with as many females as they can.

A few males, though, try a less violent approach: They show duller colors and, while the intense fighting is going on, sneak around to mate with females without doing battle at all. Make love, not war—that's their philosophy.

These guys know how to protect their eggs!

RAP SHEET

SPECIES: NORTHERN GANNET (*MORUS BASSANUS*)

PHYSICAL DESCRIPTION: LARGE WHITE BIRD WITH BLACK ON WINGS AND BUFF HEAD, 37 IN (94 CM) LONG, 6.6 LB (3 KG)

KNOWN WHEREABOUTS: NORTH AMERICAN AND EUROPEAN COASTS OF THE NORTH ATLANTIC

ALIASES: SOLAN GOOSE; EASILY MISTAKEN FOR CAPE GANNET OR AUSTRALASIAN GANNET

ANGRY BEHAVIORS: VIOLENTLY FEUDS WITH NEIGHBORS IN NESTING COLONIES

Northern Gannets roost on a cliff.

IT'S A LOVE-HATE RELATIONSHIP

Is it possible to be gregarious and antisocial at the same time? In the case of gannets, it sure seems to be. Their conflicting instincts make a gannet colony one of the angriest-looking places in the natural world.

These big seabirds make their living by fishing, and they nest in huge, dense congregations on rocky cliffs overlooking the ocean. Gannet colonies, which can encompass tens of thousands of birds, seem like scenes of barely controlled chaos, with birds continually squawking, violently feuding with neighbors, and performing ritualized displays intended to intimidate any bird that comes too close. All this reflects the gannet's need to breed near others of its kind, yet still aggressively defend the space around its nest.

PERSONAL SPACE

Gannet colonies look as if they'd been laid out by a surveyor. Each nest is precisely as far from the next as a gannet can reach with a violent thrust of its long neck and fearsome bill. Even with a demilitarized zone around each nest, it seems to a human observer that gannets waste a tremendous amount of energy on aggressive assaults, fearful that a neighbor might encroach an inch or two onto occupied territory. Gannet anger reaches its peak when two males claim the same spot, grappling and shoving until one finally gives way. All the while, there's another patch of bare rock just a couple of feet away that looks just as good as the one that caused the fight.

RAP SHEET

SPECIES: EMU (DROMAIUS NOVAEHOLLANDIAE)

PHYSICAL DESCRIPTION: LONG-LEGGED BROWNISH BIRD, UP TO 6.5 FT (2 M) TALL, 120 LB (55 KG)

KNOWN WHEREABOUTS: OPEN COUNTRY IN AUSTRALIA

ALIASES: KOOLPURRIE (ABORIGINAL)

ANGRY BEHAVIORS: KICKS WITH POWERFUL LEGS AND SHARP CLAWS

FIGHTING FOR HER MAN

Luckily for Australians, the emu isn't nearly as angry as its distant relative the cassowary. The second tallest bird in the world (after another relative, the ostrich), the flightless emu could do serious damage to humans with its strong legs and sharp claws if it was as irritable as the cassowary.

AGGRESSIVE AVIAN AUSSIE

Emus take out most of their aggression on other emus. And, in an odd role reversal, it's the female emus who battle each other for the right to mate with males, while it's the males who incubate eggs and care for the young birds. Females often inflict injuries on each other in their kicking bouts for supremacy.

You go, girl!

Stories abound of emu "attacks" on people, but the vast majority are simply manifestations of the birds' natural curiosity. An emu approaching someone is usually just checking things out, but a person facing an oncoming six-foot-tall bird is likely to find the experience a little unsettling, to say the least.

The most aggressive emu in history was actually a puppet—creatively named Emu—that appeared on British television in the 1970s. The alter ego of comedian Rod Hull, Emu attacked anyone foolhardy enough to appear on the air with it. Emu was no respecter of persons; it once ate a bouquet of flowers held by the Queen Mother. Real emus do occasionally go a little haywire, too. In the state of Georgia, police once had to use a Taser on an emu that was attacking vehicles in traffic.

Birds have been known to attack predators 100 times their size.

SCAT, CAT!

This bird tries to chase a cat out of its territory.

RAP SHEET

SPECIES: COMMON RAVEN (*CORVUS CORAX*)

PHYSICAL DESCRIPTION: ALL BLACK, 24 IN (61 CM) LONG, 2.2 LB (1 KG)

KNOWN WHEREABOUTS: MOST OF NORTH AMERICA, EUROPE, NORTHERN AFRICA, AND NORTHERN ASIA

ALIASES: CORBIE, NORTHERN RAVEN; EASILY MISTAKEN FOR CHIHUAHUAN RAVEN, AMERICAN CROW, OR CARRION CROW

ANGRY BEHAVIORS: PECKS EYES OF LAMBS AND CALVES, EATS BIRD EGGS AND NESTLINGS

Common Ravens fight over food.

BIRD OR DEVIL?

For centuries, the human race has had ambivalent feelings about the raven. The night-black bird has been deified and feared, admired for its intelligence and cursed for its guile. Symbol of life and partner with death, the raven possesses so many varied traits that people see in it what they want to see.

SMART AND SINISTER

Scientifically speaking, the raven is the world's largest songbird, yet it's more aggressive and predatory than some hawks. If there were such a thing as a bird IQ test, the raven would be in Mensa, yet its wiliness often brings it into conflict with people—when it pecks the eyes out of lambs and calves, for instance, or preys on endangered species. Because ravens often eat dead animals, the species has sometimes been seen as a go-between with the spirit world.

Native people in the Pacific Northwest admire the raven but also label it a trickster. In their mythology the bird deceived others to get what it wanted, whether food for itself or the light that it stole to illuminate the world. In Europe, ravens were thought to prophesy death; children were told that a raven would come for them if they were naughty. At the Tower of London, a legend claims that if ravens ever disappear, England will come to an end.

It's no wonder that Edgar Allan Poe chose the raven to deliver the fateful word "Nevermore" in his famous poem. What other bird has the right mix of intelligence, mystery, and melancholy? "Ghastly, gaunt, and ominous," Poe called the raven, this "thing of evil . . . bird or devil!"

RAP SHEET

SPECIES: STRIATED CARACARA
(PHALCOBOENUS AUSTRALIS)

PHYSICAL DESCRIPTION:
BLACKISH RAPTOR WITH WHITE
TAIL TIP, 25 IN (64 CM) LONG,
2.6 LB (1.2 KG)

KNOWN WHEREABOUTS:
FALKLAND ISLANDS AND SOME
ISLANDS OFF TIERRA DEL FUEGO

ALIASES: JOHNNY ROOK,
FLYING DEVIL

ANGRY BEHAVIORS: STEALS
AND DESTROYS OBJECTS

Striated Caracara
*(Phalcoboenus
australis)*

FLYING DEVILS
OF THE FALKLANDS

When Charles Darwin himself describes a bird as "quarrelsome and passionate," it's a good bet that the species qualifies as an official angry bird. It's certainly a fact that the Striated Caracara has been giving trouble to people on the Falkland Islands since the first settlers arrived in the 18th century. How much trouble? One folk name for the bird is "flying devil."

CAUGHT IN THE ACT

FALKLAND FURY

It's sheep that have brought caracaras and humans into greatest conflict. The raptors feed on dead sheep and will also attack sick and young sheep; how often caracaras kill healthy adult sheep is a matter of debate. The Striated Caracara was once officially declared a pest on the Falklands, and once ranchers killed them whenever they had the chance. Today caracaras are legally protected.

Darwin called the bird "very mischievous and inquisitive." Caracaras boldly approach people, stealing items and destroying objects seemingly just for the fun of it. A National Geographic crew working in the Falklands in 2010 discovered how much trouble caracaras can be when a group of the birds invaded the team's campsite, damaging a tent, stealing food, carrying off equipment, and strewing toilet paper all around (see "Caught in the Act"). Cameras caught the action, and it looks like the birds were enjoying themselves as they caused havoc in the camp.

Northern
Mockingbird
(Mimus polyglottos)

RAP SHEET

SPECIES: NORTHERN MOCKING-BIRD (*MIMUS POLYGLOTTOS*)

PHYSICAL DESCRIPTION: MEDIUM-SIZE SLENDER SONGBIRD, GRAY WITH WHITE PATCHES IN WINGS AND TAIL, ABOUT 10 IN (25 CM) LONG, 1.7 OZ (50 G)

KNOWN WHEREABOUTS: CONTINENTAL UNITED STATES, SOUTHERN CANADA, AND MOST OF MEXICO; NESTS IN HEDGES AND DENSE SHRUBS IN YARDS, FARM-LAND, AND DESERT SCRUB

ALIASES: MOCKER, MOCKING THRUSH

ANGRY BEHAVIORS: STRONGLY AGGRESSIVE AGAINST INTRUDERS, DIVING AND PECKING

HE NEVER *FORGETS* A FACE

Mock!

What is it with musicians and bad-boy behavior? Rock stars trash hotel rooms, and the mockingbird—one of the bird world's most renowned singers—can't seem to help getting into trouble when romance gets its hormones flowing. The mockingbird breeds across the continental United States and well down into Mexico. Because mockingbirds nest in parks, gardens, and backyards, many people have the chance to enjoy their song, as well as to observe the feisty behavior for which mockers are known.

MOCKING THEIR TERRITORY

Ing!

After the female lays her eggs, the male finds a lookout spot nearby and quickly darts out to attack anything he considers a danger: dogs, cats, hawks, and humans all risk the mockingbird's wrath if they venture too close. Even people innocently strolling down a sidewalk may find themselves victims of a surprise attack **(see "Caught in the Act")**. The U.S. Postal Service once sent letters to residents of a neighborhood in Tulsa, Oklahoma, warning them that their mail might be delayed because a mockingbird had repeatedly attacked a mail carrier over a period of several weeks.

CAUGHT IN THE ACT

One study in Florida showed that mockingbirds recognize and remember people who have repeatedly approached their nests. The male reacts more violently if he sees a repeat trespasser—even if the person wears different clothes and comes at different times of day. Who knew that little bird brains could be so perceptive?

Bird!

65

RAP SHEET

SPECIES: EUROPEAN STARLING (*STURNUS VULGARIS*)

PHYSICAL DESCRIPTION: SMALL BLACK SONGBIRD WITH BRIGHT YELLOW BILL IN BREEDING SEASON, 8 IN (21 CM) LONG, 3.2 OZ (90 G)

KNOWN WHEREABOUTS: NATIVE TO EUROPE AND PART OF ASIA; NOW INTRODUCED AROUND THE WORLD FROM NORTH AMERICA TO AUSTRALIA

ALIASES: MANY UNPRINTABLE NAMES; EASILY MISTAKEN FOR SPOTLESS STARLING

ANGRY BEHAVIORS: AGGRESSIVELY EVICTS OTHER BIRDS FROM THEIR NESTING CAVITIES

GOTCHA!

A starling evicts a Northern Flicker from its nest.

A FEATHERED
EVICTION NOTICE

What a charming idea: Way back in the 19th century, a man named Eugene Schieffelin decided that the schoolchildren of America would appreciate Shakespeare better if they could see all the kinds of birds mentioned in his plays. To get started, Schieffelin released a hundred European starlings in New York's Central Park.

The idea, though charming, was a really, really bad one. Today, more than 200 million starlings infest North America from coast to coast and from Mexico to Alaska. The bird equivalent of a noxious weed, they displaced native birds as they spread across the continent.

NOISY NUISANCE

Starlings nest in enclosed places, including in holes in trees and nest boxes put up for other birds. Highly aggressive and equally persistent, they harass other birds, chasing them away even after the victims have started nesting. Many a bird-watcher has looked on in disgust as starlings have evicted bluebirds from a nest box, or watched woodpeckers excavate a cavity in a tree only to see starlings take over when the work was finished. Two starling males sometimes fight over a nest site, with one occasionally killing the other.

All in all, it would have been a lot better if the kids reading Shakespeare's *Henry IV* had just looked up "starling" in a picture book.

RAP SHEET

NAME: CHUCK

PHYSICAL DESCRIPTION: TRIANGULAR YELLOW BIRD

ALIAS: YELLOW BIRD

HOW ANGRY IS HE: TESTY

WHAT MAKES HIM ANGRY: FEELING DISRESPECTED AND UNDERVALUED. PIGS.

ANGRY BEHAVIORS: HASTILY ATTACKING WITH A LIGHTNING-QUICK SPEED

HOBBY: SPORTS

STRONGEST ALLY: RED

YELLOW IS NOT MELLOW:
CHUCK

Floating like a butterfly and stinging like a bee, Chuck is one tough fighter who never backs down from a challenge. The pigs that incessantly steal the birds' eggs don't easily intimidate Chuck, and in fact, he is occasionally guilty of being a show-off.

CHUCK'S STORY

Even though Chuck sees himself as the best bird for the job, he doesn't feel like he gets the respect he deserves. He is a team player, always ready to strike, and is the first to support Red's ideas and strategies for attacking the pigs. He is extremely competitive and trains hard every day to be as quick and as powerful as possible. Chuck's hyperactive personality makes it hard for him to concentrate on anything for long periods of time. He quickly jumps from project to project without a moment's notice—and thus never manages to master the task at hand. Chuck often acts without thinking, which tends to lead to catastrophic results.

WHAT MAKES HIM ANGRY

Chuck feels strongly that he has to prove himself to the others, and fears that he will lose his place as Red's second in command. He suspects that Bomb (aka Black Bird) is scheming to take his place, a misconception that only fuels his competitive nature as well as his insecurities. Chuck can't see that the other birds do respect him and think he is one of the strongest birds in their group. Chuck works hard at being the best, and he gets very angry when he fails.

A Clay-colored Thrush (left) and a Great Kiskadee quarrel.

SQUAWWK! SQUAWWK!

RAP SHEET

SPECIES: GREAT KISKADEE (*PITANGUS SULPHURATUS*)

PHYSICAL DESCRIPTION: YELLOW UNDERPARTS AND BLACK-AND-WHITE STRIPED HEAD, IO IN (25 CM) LONG, 2.6 OZ (74 G)

KNOWN WHEREABOUTS: SOUTHERN TEXAS TO ARGENTINA

ALIASES: DERBY FLYCATCHER; *BIEN-TE-VEO* (SPANISH); EASILY MISTAKEN FOR LESSER KISKADEE AND BOAT-BILLED FLYCATCHER

ANGRY BEHAVIORS: ATTACKS ANY LARGE BIRD; STEALS FOOD FROM SMALL BIRDS

SMALL BIRD PACKS A
BIG PUNCH

The funhouse at an old-time carnival always had a hallway with warped mirrors that made people look way bigger than in real life. The great kiskadee seems to have looked into one and believed what it saw. Or maybe it behaves the way it does because it takes the first part of its name a little too seriously. Far from great in size, this flycatcher more than compensates in sheer ferocity.

Great kiskadees are common from southern Texas to Argentina, familiar to rural people and city dwellers alike. Their name comes from their loud *kis-ka-dee* call. Aggressive and fearless in defense of their nest, they attack almost any potential predator that appears in their territory. They've been seen not only diving at hawks but riding on their backs while vigorously whacking the raptor with their bills. Kiskadees commonly pull feathers from birds far larger than themselves, and even attack monkeys (pecking them on the head) and large snakes. They sometimes zoom up to harass vultures, which brings to mind the image of an ultralight aircraft buzzing a 747.

In keeping with their bully behavior, great kiskadees have been known to steal food and nesting material from other birds. Any way you look at it, having kiskadees in the neighborhood raises the magnitude of anger at least a couple of levels.

Red-legged
Seriema
(Cariama
cristata)

RAP SHEET

SPECIES: RED-LEGGED SERIEMA
(*CARIAMA CRISTATA*)

PHYSICAL DESCRIPTION: LONG-
LEGGED GRAYISH BIRD, 30 IN (76
CM) LONG, 3.3 LB (1.5 KG)

KNOWN WHEREABOUTS:
GRASSLANDS OF SOUTH AMERICA

ALIASES: CRESTED CARIAMA

ANGRY BEHAVIORS: RIPS PREY
APART WITH "VELOCIRAPTOR"
CLAW

TERROR BIRD

In the grasslands of South America roams a ferocious predatory bird that's quick to pounce on and kill its prey with a sharp-pointed bill and claws specially shaped to tear animals apart. Luckily for anyone living in the area, the Red-legged Seriema is only about the size of a skinny, long-legged chicken, and its prey is mostly small rodents, lizards, insects, and snakes.

Other creatures are lucky they didn't live a few million years ago, because the seriema is the only living relative of birds that once ranked among the deadliest predators ever to walk the Earth—"terror birds." Looking something like ostriches, only with monstrous eaglelike bills, terror birds (or Phorusrhacids) stood up to ten feet tall, ran as fast as a racehorse, and killed prey with blows from their massive beaks.

NO MERCY

Seriemas carry on the tradition of their long-ago ancestors, grabbing prey animals in their bills and smashing them against rocks to stun them, then using a curved claw no other bird has—very much like the weapon wielded by velociraptor dinosaurs—to rip them apart before swallowing the pieces. In other words, the seriema behaves like a miniature predatory dinosaur.

South Americans who have chickens or other poultry sometimes catch young seriemas and keep them around to give the alarm when predators approach. Not only are seriemas fierce, they're extremely vigilant, and their warning cries—something like a war chant—can be heard for a mile or more.

When courting, male Black-shouldered Kites feed their mates in midair.

AAAAAAR

Black-shouldered Kite (*Elanus caeruleus*)

GH!

Masked
Lapwing
(*Vanellus
miles*)

I GOT MAD KNIFE SKILLS.

RAP SHEET

SPECIES: MASKED LAPWING (*VANELLUS MILES*)

PHYSICAL DESCRIPTION: MEDIUM-SIZE BIRD, BROWN ABOVE, WHITE BELOW, WITH YELLOW FACE; 14 IN (35 CM) LONG, 14 OZ (400 G)

KNOWN WHEREABOUTS: AUSTRALIA, NEW GUINEA, AND NEW ZEALAND

ALIASES: SPUR-WINGED PLOVER, SPUR-WINGED LAPWING

ANGRY BEHAVIORS: SCREAMS AND DIVES AT PEOPLE NEAR ITS NEST

CAREFUL!
HE'S GOT A KNIFE

It's one thing for an angry bird to dive at you and give you a peck with its bill. It's a whole different thing for a bird to be carrying a dagger—one in each hand, in fact.

The Masked Lapwing nests on the ground in open areas such as playgrounds, golf courses, and parking lots. This means that a breeding pair often comes into close contact with people. Highly territorial, these birds call loudly and pretend to be injured to lure an intruder away from their nest. They're great actors, too; watching a lapwing struggle along the ground, you'd swear it had a broken wing. If that ruse doesn't work, they'll swoop at whatever is causing them distress, whether it's another bird, a dog, or a person.

ARMED AND DANGEROUS

Curiously, Masked Lapwings have a sharp spur, like a tiny knife, protruding from the bend of each wing. The spur's function is debated, but the lapwings probably use the weapon in fighting with rival lapwings over mates or territory, and possibly in defending their nests and young against predators.

The old folklore that the lapwing's spur can inject poison is just a myth, but getting dive-bombed by a hostile bird can be scary. While most attacks are just bluffs, the swooping bird occasionally comes into contact with the swoopee, causing scratches or bruises. In any case, it's better to avoid a confrontation with a bird that's armed and dangerous.

Egyptian Goose
(Alopochen aegyptiaca)

HONNNNNK!

THIS BEAUTY REALLY IS
A BEAST

The Egyptian Goose is one of the world's most attractive waterfowl, with plumage in shades of brown, a striking chestnut eye patch, and wings in gleaming white and iridescent green. Its beauty has seduced a great many people—nearly all of whom have later regretted ever getting to know this maniacally aggressive bird.

In their native Africa, Egyptian Geese have long been known for their willingness to fight anything and everything, from other waterbirds to eagles, even crocodiles that intrude on their territory. How pugnacious are they? Famed animal behaviorist Konrad Lorenz wrote extensively about "the fighting urge of the Egyptian goose, which often seems insane to the observer."

OUTRAGED ORNAMENTS

Egyptian Geese were brought to England in the 17th century as "ornamental" birds for the lakes of country estates. Unfortunately, they brought their violent nature with them. They drive away other birds and sometimes charge at people who come near. In places, they have attacked ospreys—a threatened raptor species making a comeback in the British Isles—and stolen their nesting sites. Especially in southern England, many parks, golf courses, housing developments, and recreational sites have seen a virtual plague of Egyptian Geese. The population has grown so large in England,

Continued on p. 80

and the birds have become such nuisances, that the government declared the species an official pest in 2009.

In South Africa, the Egyptian Goose is despised not only for its aggressiveness toward other birds but also for eating farmers' crops. Its striking appearance still tempts some people to raise the Egyptian Goose as a domestic fowl, even though one leading poultry guidebook warns that it is "the most aggressive and bad-tempered of all breeds during the breeding season." In many places around the world, it is now illegal to import Egyptian Geese or release them into the wild.

Female Egyptian Geese are well known for inciting their mates into violent rages in which the males attack any other males of the same species nearby—or, if none are around, any other bird of any sort. When two Egyptian Goose males fight, the female watches without helping her mate. If he wins, the pair share a "triumph ceremony" that helps strengthen their bond with each other. If he loses, in the words of Lorenz, "she is always ready to go over with flying colors to the side of the winner."

RAP SHEET

SPECIES: EGYPTIAN GOOSE (ALOPOCHEN AEGYPTIACA)

PHYSICAL DESCRIPTION: BROWN-ISH WITH GREEN-AND-WHITE WINGS, 29 IN (74 CM) LONG, 4.6 LB (2.1 KG)

KNOWN WHEREABOUTS: SOUTHERN AFRICA; INTRODUCED INTO EUROPE

ALIASES: GOES BY GOOSE, BUT REALLY IS A SHELDUCK

ANGRY BEHAVIORS: BITES, HITS WITH WINGS, KICKS

Two
Egyptian
Geese chase
each other.

81

A Eurasian Coot attacks an intruder coot.

RAP SHEET

SPECIES: EURASIAN COOT (*FULICA ATRA*)

PHYSICAL DESCRIPTION: DUCK-LIKE BLACK WATERBIRD, 15 IN (38 CM) LONG

KNOWN WHEREABOUTS: MUCH OF EUROPE, ASIA, AFRICA, AND AUSTRALASIA

ALIASES: BALD COOT, BLACK DIVER, WATER CROW

ANGRY BEHAVIORS: CHARGES, KICKS, AND PECKS

OLD COOT HAS A MEAN TEMPER

If you've ever wondered why people call a cranky, ill-tempered codger an "old coot," all you have to do is spend a little time watching real coots. There aren't many creatures more irritable, hostile, violent, and just plain mean than these small black waterbirds.

DON'T CROSS A COOT

Coots spend their time on or near water, and they most definitely don't like to share their space. When an intruder appears, a coot raises its wings and puffs up its feathers to appear as large as possible, then lowers its head and charges. Other coots, ducks, turtles, snakes, and even people in canoes can push a coot's hot button—it goes from placid to angry in a heartbeat. But coots aren't stupid; they don't risk injury by attacking big birds such as swans or pelicans.

Coots often gang up on a newcomer in their territory, striking the intruder often until it's exhausted. The assailants hold it underwater until it drowns. Violence must be in this bird's genes; young coots begin acting aggressive toward other birds when they're only a few days old.

Female coots may lay a dozen or more eggs, which hatch successively over a period of several days. Once the adults have about eight young, though, they simply ignore the rest of the eggs, letting the developing embryos die in their shells. It seems cold-hearted, but it's a way to make sure that the living young get enough parental care and food.

LEVEL 3 OUTRAGED

(adj.) aroused to anger or resentment in usually by some grave offense

Bald Eagle
(*Haliaeetus leucocephalus*)

RAP SHEET

NAME: BOMB

PHYSICAL DESCRIPTION: ROUND, BLACK BIRD; TURNS RED WHEN VERY ANGRY

ALIAS: BLACK BIRD

HOW ANGRY IS HE: OUTRAGED

WHAT MAKES HIM ANGRY: INTERRUPTIONS IN HIS DAILY SCHEDULE. PIGS.

ANGRY BEHAVIORS: IMMEDIATELY ELIMINATING THE ENEMY BY BLOWING UP WITH ANGER

HOBBY: CALLIGRAPHY

STRONGEST ALLIES: MATILDA AND RED

TICK, TICK, TICK, BOOM: BOMB

When you have a short fuse it's best to keep things organized and predictable, and that's exactly how Bomb keeps his temper under control . . . most of the time. Totally fearless and quick to take action, Bomb is the strongest of the Angry Birds but the worst at controlling his temper.

BOMB'S STORY

In an attempt to control his anger, Bomb has created a daily routine in hopes that a structured life will bring about peace and balance. Unfortunately, when things go awry (even something as simple as his ice cream melting and falling off the cone), he explodes with rage. Chuck (aka Yellow Bird) usually pushes him over the edge with unnecessary (and unplanned) tests of strength. The other birds do their best to make sure he stays on schedule, but this babying annoys Bomb even more. He just wants to be treated normally. Besides his schedule Bomb uses other tactics to stay calm: soaking in the hot Zen springs, taking soothing walks through the meadows, smelling the flowers. Even though he finds them disgusting, Bomb tries the herbal calming remedies favored by Matilda (aka White Bird) in hopes that there might be an all-natural solution to his explosive behavior.

WHAT MAKES HIM ANGRY

The pigs' constant robbing of the eggs and the general warlike atmosphere that surrounds the birds really aggravate Bomb and drive him to take refuge in his routines. If the pigs do appear, Bomb likes to eliminate the enemy immediately. This allows him to get back to his routines without too much interruption. It's a vicious cycle when the pigs disturb his routines because not only is Bomb angry toward the pigs but the unscheduled interruption fuels his anger even more.

A Kea nibbles on a car's windshield wiper.

RAP SHEET

SPECIES: KEA *(NESTOR NOTABILIS)*

PHYSICAL DESCRIPTION: LARGE PARROT, MOSTLY OLIVE GREEN, WITH RED RUMP AND UNDER-WINGS; LONG, STRONGLY HOOKED BILL; 18 IN (46 CM) LONG, 2.1 LB (0.95 KG)

KNOWN WHEREABOUTS: SOUTH ISLAND OF NEW ZEALAND, IN THE HIGH MOUNTAINS OF THE SOUTH-ERN ALPS AND NEARBY FOOTHILLS

ALIASES: EASILY MISTAKEN FOR THE NEW ZEALAND KAKA

ANGRY BEHAVIORS: CHEWS UP OR STEALS OBJECTS AND HAS BEEN KNOWN TO ATTACK SHEEP

MMMMM, TASTES LIKE MAYHEM.

DON'T TURN YOUR BACK!

Where do parrots live? In hot spots with palm trees and rain forests, most people would probably say. But the tropics aren't the only home for these colorful, intelligent birds. Travelers in New Zealand's snowy Southern Alps are almost certain to come into contact with the big green parrots called Keas—and that contact could be highly unpleasant.

A TASTE FOR DESTRUCTION

One of the world's few high-elevation parrots, the inquisitive Kea loves to check out people and their stuff, and its curiosity often turns destructive. Countless visitors have returned from a hike to find that Keas have chewed the rubber off the windshield wipers of their car or broken the radio antenna. Skiers who leave their skis unattended may discover that parrots have damaged the bindings. Careless campers who leave gear outside their tents in Kea country may awake to find various possessions missing—stolen by Keas. Keas are strong enough to carry off a hiking boot, which means real trouble for backpackers in the middle of the Fiordland wilderness. Who wants to hop back to the trailhead on one foot?

Hotels in the Southern Alps place warning notes in guest rooms: "Do not leave any articles of furniture or clothing on your balcony as the Kea will not hesitate to destroy the items." Highly social, Keas make even more mischief by traveling in groups. New Zealand ranchers once commonly shot Keas, believing them to be sheep killers. In fact, until 1971 the country offered a legal bounty on the birds. Keas are now protected by law, but poaching continues, and the species is now considered endangered.

I'M THE THUNDER FROM DOWN UNDER!

Noisy Miner
(Manorina melanocephala)

RAP SHEET

SPECIES: NOISY MINER (MANORINA MELANOCEPHALA)

PHYSICAL DESCRIPTION: MOSTLY GRAY WITH BLACK "MASK," 10 IN (25 CM) LONG, 2.5 OZ (70 G)

KNOWN WHEREABOUTS: EASTERN AUSTRALIA

ALIASES: SOLDIER BIRD; MICKEY; EASILY MISTAKEN FOR YELLOW-THROATED MINER OR BLACK-EARED MINER

ANGRY BEHAVIORS: HARASSES AND DISPLACES OTHER SPECIES

URBAN BIRD GANGS TERRORIZE AUSTRALIA

Bird thugs take over Australian cities! It sounds like a tabloid headline, but it's true. The Noisy Miner loves the environment people have created in our neighborhoods, but it hates other birds. When bullying flocks of Noisy Miners invade an area, other birds have to move out. These "street gangs" (as one ecologist has called them) won't tolerate anybody else on their turf.

NEIGHBORHOOD NUISANCE

Noisy Miners are native to most of eastern Australia, but their numbers have skyrocketed in recent decades. The reason? They thrive in the kinds of habitats that people create: cutover forests, woodlands with underbrush removed, parks with lots of open areas, and suburban landscaping. The problem? These birds are both highly aggressive and extremely intolerant of other birds—of any species. When populations of Noisy Miners go up, other birds disappear. Miners also harass dogs and cats and have injured people by diving and pecking at their faces. (And did we mention that Noisy Miners are extremely noisy?)

Ecologists worry about the loss of biodiversity caused when miners displace other birdlife. For example, when insect-eating birds vanish, trees suffer from pests and many die. Some people think the only real way to restore Australia's ecological balance is to kill large numbers of Noisy Miners. Such plans are controversial, so for now gangs of Noisy Miners are still free to kick other birds out of their homes.

||||||||||||||||||||||||||||||||||||||||||||||||||||||||||||||||||||||||||||||||||||||||||||||||||||||||||

Canada Goose
(*Branta canadensis*)

OUTTA MY WAY! THIS SCHOOL'S MINE!

RAP SHEET

SPECIES: CANADA GOOSE (*BRANTA CANADENSIS*)

PHYSICAL DESCRIPTION: TAN BODY WITH BLACK NECK AND WHITE CHEEKS, 45 IN (114 CM) LONG WITH WINGSPAN UP TO 6 FT (1.9 M), 12.5 LB (5.6 KG)

KNOWN WHEREABOUTS: NORTH AMERICA; INTRODUCED IN NORTHERN EUROPE

ALIASES: EASILY MISTAKEN FOR CACKLING GOOSE

ANGRY BEHAVIORS: HISSING, CHARGING, PECKING, AND BITING

ANGRY BIRD ON CAMPUS

There are many things to fear about going to college—cafeteria food, a smelly roommate, an 8 a.m. class across campus—but for students of Northern Illinois University, the most intimidating part of their educational experience has been an angry Canada Goose.

CANTANKEROUS CANADIAN

Students walking near Chick Evans Field House have been menaced, hissed at, and even chased by the goose, which sprints across the ground to confront "trespassers." One student said the bird shows special aggression toward particular people. "It hisses at me every day," the freshman says. "It tries to bite me every day." Despite the trouble it causes, the goose was given its own Facebook page by students, who share their encounters with the cranky critter.

CAUGHT IN THE ACT

Attacks have become common as Canada Geese have invaded parks and golf courses. Not only do these big birds leave stinky messes everywhere, the males become highly aggressive in nesting season. The problem gets worse when people feed the geese, causing them to lose their fear of humans. Passersby have suffered scratches, bruises, and even broken bones in goose attacks (see "Caught in the Act").

If confronted, experts say, you should maintain eye contact and avoid showing fear while slowly backing away. That's hard to do when a 15-pound gander charges you with anger in its eyes.

Most of the time, albatross prefer to stay at sea, and come ashore only to mate and raise their young.

94

A Campbell
Black-browed
Albatross
prepares
to land.

HEY! I'M WALKIN' HERE.

A Wild Turkey crosses the sidewalk to a passerby's dismay.

TURKEYS STRIKE BACK

The Bald Eagle is a fierce-looking bird, everyone would agree. But Benjamin Franklin didn't want it as a symbol of the United States, calling it "a Bird of bad moral Character" and "a rank Coward." Franklin's preference was the Wild Turkey, which he called "a much more respectable Bird . . . a Bird of Courage."

Lately, residents of suburban America have been finding the Wild Turkey a little too courageous. After decades when the turkey population declined because of overhunting, these big fowl have been invading neighborhoods across the country, staking claims to yards and parks and terrorizing runners, postal workers, motorists, and even people just walking out to their mailbox (see "Caught in the Act").

Okay—when it comes to intimidation, a turkey isn't exactly a charging rhinoceros. But males can stand up to four feet tall and weigh more than 20 pounds, and an aggressive bird can do some damage by kicking with strong legs and sharp claws.

CAUGHT IN THE ACT

SWEET REVENGE

In Sacramento, California, a television news producer heard about a flock of turkeys that had been attacking joggers in a local neighborhood, so she went to have a look for herself. One of the birds chased her down the street for more than 90 seconds and trapped her in her car, ignoring her squeals of "Oh my God!" and "Leave me alone!" The resulting video went viral, making a star of "Terrible Tom" and his victim.

Continued on p. 98

Another viral turkey-attack video showed a fowl chasing a U.S. Postal Service van down a street on Cape Cod in Massachusetts, keeping pace at speeds up to 25 miles per hour. The bird repeatedly hurled itself against the door, as if desperate to attack the driver. But maybe it just had a letter it wanted picked up.

Similar stories abound across the country. Staten Island, New York, suffered a turkey invasion in 2011 that drew complaints from dozens of households. The birds caused traffic jams, ate seeds people planted in their gardens, and even stole cookies right out of the hands of children. (You can't get much more shameful than that.) On Martha's Vineyard in Massachusetts, turkeys terrorized residents, and one male bird (also, inevitably, named Tom) even attacked a police officer who went to investigate. The cop shot the turkey, causing a bit of controversy among those who felt the death penalty wasn't warranted.

RAP SHEET

SPECIES: WILD TURKEY
(MELEAGRIS GALLOPAVO)

PHYSICAL DESCRIPTION: BULKY BROWN BIRD, UP TO 4 FT (1.2 M) TALL, 22 LB (9.9 KG); FEMALES ARE SMALLER, 12 LB (5.4 KG)

KNOWN WHEREABOUTS: MOST OF THE UNITED STATES AND PARTS OF CANADA AND MEXICO

ALIASES: TOM TURKEY, GOBBLER, THANKSGIVING DINNER

ANGRY BEHAVIORS: CHASES PEOPLE, KICKS AND SCRATCHES

What makes turkeys so aggressive, so manic, so stubborn? Let's not forget that Franklin also admitted the bird was "a little vain & silly." He might have added "a little stupid," too.

|||||||||||||||||||||||||||||||||||||||||||||||||||||

That's one tough turkey!

Wild Turkey
(*Meleagris
gallopavo*)

A Herring Gull attacks an innocent bystander.

RAP SHEET

SPECIES: HERRING GULL (*LARUS ARGENTATUS*)

PHYSICAL DESCRIPTION: MOSTLY WHITE WITH GRAY WINGS AND BACK, 24 IN (61 CM) LONG, 2.4 LB (1.1 KG)

KNOWN WHEREABOUTS: NORTHERN EUROPE AND EASTERN NORTH AMERICA

ALIASES: SEAGULL; EASILY MISTAKEN FOR YELLOW-LEGGED GULL AND THAYER'S GULL

ANGRY BEHAVIORS: HARASSING PEOPLE FOR FOOD, PECKING

REAL-LIFE HORROR FILM

People sometimes imagine themselves in a movie scene, but it's usually a romance or adventure story—not an Alfred Hitchcock horror film. Yet a woman in a southwestern England resort town found herself in just such a scary situation when she was attacked by a gull.

GULL-ING IN FOR THE ATTACK

The 36-year-old woman was walking along the seashore in Burnham-on-Sea when a gull dived and pecked her head with its bill, causing three bloody puncture wounds that required a trip to the hospital. An official said the incident was "terrifying" for the woman. Recalling Hitchcock's classic film *The Birds*, he said, "Here it is actually happening." Many gull-human confrontations had occurred in the area earlier—birds stealing food from tourists and postal workers attacked—but none had been so violent.

There's more to the story, as well. Three years before, a local wildlife group had warned that some residents had been shooting troublesome gulls with air rifles. Several wounded birds had been brought to a local wildlife rescue center and found to have pellets imbedded in their bodies.

Were the gulls out for revenge against people? Probably not. Birds aren't known for their reasoning and long-term planning abilities. And Hitchcock would no doubt have rejected revenge as a plot point in *The Birds*. One of the eeriest things about the film was the mystery surrounding the birds' motive for violence. The movie ends on an unsettling note, with the main characters fleeing while massive flocks continue to gather for more attacks.

RAP SHEET

SPECIES: NAZCA BOOBY (*SULA GRANTI*)

PHYSICAL DESCRIPTION: MOSTLY WHITE WITH BLACK ON WINGS AND TAIL, 32 IN (81 CM) LONG, 4.1 LB (1.9 KG)

KNOWN WHEREABOUTS: GALÁPAGOS ISLANDS AND SOME PACIFIC MEXICAN ISLANDS

ALIASES: EASILY MISTAKEN FOR MASKED BOOBY

ANGRY BEHAVIORS: CHICKS KILL SIBLINGS; UNMATED ADULTS ABUSE YOUNG BIRDS

BACK OFF, BOOBY.

An adult Nazca Booby and chick

VICIOUS VIOLENT CYCLE

Child abuse occurs in more species than just humans. As sad as it is to behold, the mistreatment of young birds in one tropical species may provide important clues to help combat abusive human behavior.

The Nazca Booby is a seabird that nests in large colonies in the Galápagos Islands, where each mated pair raises a single chick. (If two chicks hatch, the stronger one kills its sibling—the "insurance egg" method of making sure at least one young bird is successfully raised.) To find enough food for their chick, both adults often leave the nest at the same time to go fishing. While they're gone, unmated adult boobies look for unattended young birds and interact with them aggressively.

AVIAN ABUSE

A study in the ornithological journal *The Auk* showed that young birds that suffered mistreatment were far more likely to commit abuse as adults. Because the adults mistreating young were not related to their victims, the transmission of abusive behavior was not genetic, but somehow "social."

Significantly, this was the first time such behavior was shown to be socially transmitted from one generation to another in an animal other than humans. Scientists proposed that it might help understand the "cycle of violence" in humans, in which children who are abused grow up to be abusers. Much more study is needed, but investigations could help us eliminate the trauma of abuse directed at children.

RAP SHEET

NAME: MIGHTY EAGLE

PHYSICAL DESCRIPTION: MYSTERIOUS, SELDOM SEEN GIGANTIC BIRD OF PREY

ALIAS: MIGHTY

HOW ANGRY IS HE: OUTRAGED

WHAT MAKES HIM ANGRY: INTRUDERS. PIGS.

ANGRY BEHAVIORS: TOTAL ANNIHILATION OF ANYTHING IN HIS WAY. TRIGGERED BY SARDINES

HOBBY: HISTORY

STRONGEST ALLIES: THE BLUES

A VANQUISHED HERO:
MIGHTY EAGLE

Armed with an unbelievable knowledge of pig weaknesses, Mighty Eagle is one of the greatest heroes of the war with the pigs. But one harrowing incident sent him into self-imposed exile on a mountaintop. On his watch, the pigs were able to steal the eggs, and Mighty Eagle's failure to protect them shamed him so much that he retreated into solitude.

MIGHTY EAGLE'S STORY

Due to long exile Mighty Eagle feels utterly useless and believes that the other birds feel the same way. He also believes that Red is avoiding him purposely and will never forgive him for his mistake. The only interaction Mighty Eagle has with the bunch is with the Blues, who act as mediators between him and the rest of the older birds. The Blues bring him sardines (his favorite!) to persuade him to tell his legendary tales and war stories, and to get him to help—occasionally—when the birds need him. Mighty Eagle would love to return to the bunch and redeem himself, but his shame and fear of rejection keep him from making the first move.

WHAT MAKES HIM ANGRY

Out of old habit Mighty Eagle hates the pigs. But ever since he slipped into isolation, he takes out his anger on anything that disturbs his peace. His isolation has turned him into a grumpy hermit who drives everyone away. He allows the Blues to visit him because they listen to his stories about his glory days, and besides, they bring his favorite—the sardines!

PEEK-A-BOO. I'LL PECK YOU!

Eurasian Capercaillie (*Tetrao urogallus*)

RAP SHEET

SPECIES: EURASIAN CAPERCAILLIE (*TETRAO UROGALLUS*)

PHYSICAL DESCRIPTION: MALES MOSTLY BLACK, 35 IN (90 CM) LONG, 9.5 LB (4.3 KG); FEMALES BROWN AND SMALLER, 4.5 LB (2 KG)

KNOWN WHEREABOUTS: NORTHERN EUROPE AND ASIA

ALIASES: COCK OF THE WOOD, WOOD GROUSE

ANGRY BEHAVIORS: AGGRESSIVELY CHARGES AND PECKS INTRUDERS AND RIVALS

KING OF THE FOREST

Animals don't threaten travelers in the cold forests of northern Europe much anymore. The wolves and bears of folklore have largely disappeared, and the only poisonous snake isn't very dangerous at all. So what's left for hikers in the forest to worry about?

A huge, angry bird called the capercaillie, that's what. The world's largest grouse, this stocky black bird can be 35 inches (90 cm) long and weigh up to 14 pounds (6.4 kg). Normally shy, the male in spring becomes highly pugnacious, making weird popping and belching calls and charging at anything that comes near. The courting bird spreads his tail, points his bill at the sky, and puffs up his fluffy neck feathers, making himself look as fearsome as possible.

CAUGHT IN THE ACT

These male capercaillies will attack anything from sheep to pigs to humans to automobiles. Many a hiker, cross-country skier, or mountain biker has been charged by a capercaillie in the forest, forced to back away while frantically searching for a limb or other defensive weapon (see "Caught in the Act").

CELEBRITY CHALLENGE

The most famous capercaillie attack involved none other than famed British naturalist and filmmaker Sir David Attenborough. While filming his series *The Life of Birds*, Sir David was charged by an aggressive male, pushed backwards, and knocked over—the whole incident captured on tape. Capercaillie attacks, while sometimes scary, aren't really dangerous, except to other capercaillies.

Two Blue Jays fight with each other.

RAP SHEET

SPECIES: BLUE JAY (CYANOCITTA CRISTATA)

PHYSICAL DESCRIPTION: MEDIUM-SIZE SONGBIRD, MOSTLY BLUE WITH WHITE AND BLACK MARKINGS, 11 IN (28 CM) LONG, 2.5 OZ (72 G)

KNOWN WHEREABOUTS: EASTERN AND CENTRAL NORTH AMERICA

ALIASES: JAYBIRD, CORN-THIEF

ANGRY BEHAVIORS: RAUCOUS ALARM CALLS; LOUDLY "MOBBING" PREDATORS

ANGRY BIRD GETS BAD RAP

Big.

Everybody knew somebody in school like the Blue Jay: a little too flashy and smart for his own good, and more than a little bit of a troublemaker. You figure he's got to be up to something wicked all the time.

HE WAS FRAMED

Look at John James Audubon's famous painting of Blue Jays. He shows three of them caught red-handed eating the eggs of a smaller bird. For decades people saw the painting and thought, Egg thief! Baby bird killer! Back when people debated whether birds were good or bad, the Blue Jay was unquestionably a bad guy.

Blue.

A 1947 scientific article said the Blue Jay "gives us the impression of being independent, lawless, haughty, even impudent . . . His mercurial temper, always just below the boiling point, is ever ready to flare up into rage and screaming attack." At a feeder, a Blue Jay swoops in, scattering sparrows and finches and taking the food for itself. But when there's a hawk, snake, or cat around, the Blue Jay loudly sounds the alarm, warning the neighborhood of danger.

Bullies.

If you asked bird-watchers to name their favorites, the Blue Jay would show up on most lists. They can be loud, temperamental, and overbearing at times, but backyards would be a lot less lively without their angry personality.

Harpy Eagle
(*Harpia harpyja*)

RAP SHEET

SPECIES: HARPY EAGLE
(*HARPIA HARPYJA*)

PHYSICAL DESCRIPTION: LARGE
GRAY-AND-WHITE RAPTOR, 40 IN
(101 CM) LONG WITH WINGSPAN
OF 6.5 FT (2 M); FEMALES 16.5 LB
(7.5 KG), MALES 10 LB (4.5 KG)

KNOWN WHEREABOUTS: CEN-
TRAL AND SOUTH AMERICA

ALIASES: EASILY MISTAKEN
FOR THE CRESTED EAGLE

ANGRY BEHAVIORS:
USES MASSIVE
TALONS TO PREY
ON RAIN FOREST
ANIMALS

FIERCE RULER OF THE AMAZON SKY

In every jungle, there can be only one king, and for the birds of Amazonia, there's no doubt who it is: the awe-inspiring Harpy Eagle. Weighing up to 20 pounds, with powerful legs and huge, sharp talons, this fierce predator is a nightmare on wings for sloths, monkeys, opossums, and other potential victims of its hunting flights. Through much of Central and South America, the Harpy Eagle truly rules the rain forest sky.

Unlike other eagles that soar high on long wings, the Harpy has relatively short wings that it uses to zoom through the forest canopy, snatching prey from tree limbs. One scientist in Brazil watched in amazement as a Harpy captured a male howler monkey weighing an estimated 14 pounds. Harpy Eagles are also strong enough to kill young deer.

LOOKS TOUGH, ACTS TOUGH

In 2010, a BBC film crew got a firsthand look at just how aggressive a Harpy can be. Making a documentary in Venezuela, the crew set up a camera in a tree near a nest. As a cameraman ascended the tree, a Harpy dived at and struck him repeatedly. Once, the eagle hit the cameraman so hard that it knocked away his microphone and momentarily stunned him.

Harpy Eagles are rare because of destruction of their rain forest habitat, but you can get an idea of its appearance by watching a Harry Potter movie. Designers used the Harpy as the inspiration for Fawkes the Phoenix, Dumbledore's magical pet bird.

European Starlings decorate a van with droppings.

The white material in bird droppings is not feces, but urine.

A pair of Parasitic Jaegers steal fish from an Arctic Tern.

STOP! THIEVES!

RAP SHEET

SPECIES: PARASITIC JAEGER (*STERCORARIUS PARASITICUS*)

PHYSICAL DESCRIPTION: MEDIUM-SIZE SEABIRD, VARIABLY BROWNISH WITH LIGHTER UNDERPARTS, 19 IN (48 CM) LONG, 1.1 LB (0.5 KG)

KNOWN WHEREABOUTS: BREEDS IN ARCTIC AREAS

ALIASES: ARCTIC SKUA; EASILY MISTAKEN FOR LONG-TAILED JAEGER OR POMARINE JAEGER

ANGRY BEHAVIORS: STEALS FOOD FROM OTHER BIRDS

AN ARRRRGRESSIVE BIRD

Pirate, parasite, scavenger, hunter, robber—with descriptions like those, it's no wonder that, as one naturalist wrote, all its neighbors "cordially hate the jaeger." Imagine that you'd just sat down with a sandwich for lunch when somebody came along and grabbed it out of your hands. You'd hate the thief, too, wouldn't you?

THEFT BY NATURE

The Parasitic Jaeger (*jaeger* is German for "hunter") is essentially a gull that's evolved into a hawklike predator. Where it breeds in the Arctic, it steals eggs and nestlings from other birds; pairs of jaegers also team up to hunt and kill birds, some larger than themselves. But the Parasitic Jaeger earned its reputation as a pirate for robbing other birds. Jaegers watch gulls and terns, looking for one that's caught a fish. Then, using its powerful flight, the jaeger zooms in to harass its victim, chasing relentlessly until the other bird drops its meal.

On their breeding grounds, jaegers pugnaciously and fearlessly attack any intruder, including eagles, owls, foxes, caribou, and humans. A person approaching a jaeger nest is likely to be attacked from behind, getting a whack on the head from an angry parent.

After nesting season, Parasitic Jaegers fly all the way to the Southern Hemisphere, where it's summer and seabirds are nesting in large colonies. There, jaegers get all their food by theft, much of it stolen from parent birds carrying fish back to their nests to feed their young. If there's nobody around to rob, jaegers will scavenge any old dead thing washed up on shore, "for nothing in the line of food, however putrid it may be, seems to miss the mark of their rapacious appetites," as one observer wrote.

WHO YOU CALLING UGLY?

Looks aren't everything, you know.

RAP SHEET

SPECIES: LAPPET-FACED VULTURE (*TORGOS TRACHELIOTUS*)

PHYSICAL DESCRIPTION: BLACKISH-BROWN BODY, 45 IN (114 CM) LONG WITH WINGSPAN OF 9 FT (2.8 M), 21 LB (9.4 KG)

KNOWN WHEREABOUTS: SOUTHERN AFRICA

ALIASES: AFRICAN EARED VULTURE; EASILY MISTAKEN FOR WHITE-HEADED VULTURE

ANGRY BEHAVIORS: DOMINATES OTHER SCAVENGERS AT PREDATOR KILLS

A Lappet-Faced Vulture (right) attacks a Rüppell's Vulture.

BIG, UGLY—AND MEAN

There's a cartoon that shows two vultures perched on a tree in the desert, with one saying, "To heck with patience. Let's go kill something." More than most of its relatives, the Lappet-faced Vulture of southern Africa lives by this predatory philosophy.

The Lappet-faced gets most of its food from carrion, such as large animals killed by lions and other predators. But this huge, powerful vulture has been known to take living prey up to the size of flamingos and young antelopes. The Lappet-faced isn't nearly as fast and agile as eagles or falcons, but it's simply so big that few birds can resist when it decides to make a snack of their eggs or nestlings.

LOOKS THAT CAN KILL

Soaring high on wings that span nine feet, the Lappet-faced Vulture scans the countryside for signs of a predator kill. Other scavengers may get there first, but when the Lappet-faced arrives, its aggressiveness makes it the boss. The Lappet-faced spreads its wings (to seem even bigger than it is) and charges to chase away jackals. Even cheetahs will back down rather than face an attacking Lappet-faced.

This species has a massive bill with sharp cutting edges that it uses to tear into the tough hides of animals such as wildebeest, which smaller birds can't slice open. In this way, the Lappet-faced Vulture actually benefits other scavengers. No vulture is going to win a beauty contest, but the Lappet-faced is especially macabre. In fact, South African ornithologist E. Leonard Gill described it as "one of the most hideous birds in the world."

Yuck.

RAP SHEET

SPECIES: NORTHERN FULMAR (*FULMARUS GLACIALIS*)

PHYSICAL DESCRIPTION: PLUMAGE VARIES FROM GRAY TO WHITE, 19 IN (48 CM) LONG WITH WINGSPAN OF 42 IN (107 CM), 1.5 LB (0.7 KG)

KNOWN WHEREABOUTS: NORTHERN OCEANS WORLDWIDE

ALIASES: ARCTIC FULMAR; EASILY MISTAKEN FOR SOUTHERN FULMAR

ANGRY BEHAVIORS: KILLS BY VOMITING STOMACH OIL

A Northern Fulmar chick expels poisonous bile.

STOP RIGHT THERE
OR I'LL . . . VOMIT?

Birds under attack have several ways to defend themselves: pointed beaks, powerful legs, sharp claws, and . . . deadly barf? Is there really a bird that carries a liquid weapon in its stomach?

Yes, an angry Northern Fulmar can kill other animals by retching—a really gross but highly effective defensive tactic that's used even by young birds still in the nest. The fulmar, a gull-like seabird, can accurately aim a stream of stinky stomach oil at targets up to six feet away and has the ability to expel barf bombs several times before running out of ammunition.

The victim of a fulmar vomit volley suffers the same fate as a bird soaked by an oil spill: matted feathers and an inability to repel water and insulate. Unable to fly, swim, or stay warm, the drenched bird often dies. While most of its victims are other birds (up to the size of owls), fulmars have also killed rabbits that were burrowing where they wanted to nest.

LIFE-SUSTAINING VOMIT

The yellowish, irritating, foul-smelling oil derives from the fulmar's diet of fish, shrimp, and other sea creatures. A rich energy source, the oil also provides emergency food for the fulmar if bad weather keeps it from hunting. Biologists, understandably, wear rain gear when studying fulmars. While the oil wouldn't kill a human, getting sprayed by an angry fulmar would almost certainly be the worst thing to happen to you all week.

LEVEL 4 — FURIOUS

(adj.) exhibiting ferocious displays of anger

Australasian
Gannet
(*Morus
serrator*)

Mississippi Kite (*Ictinia mississippiensis*)

FORRRRRRE!

RAP SHEET

SPECIES: MISSISSIPPI KITE (*ICTINIA MISSISSIPPIENSIS*)

PHYSICAL DESCRIPTION: PALE GRAY WITH DARKER WINGS AND TAIL, 15 IN (38 CM) LONG, 10.5 OZ (300 G)

KNOWN WHEREABOUTS: NESTS IN SOUTHEASTERN AND SOUTH-CENTRAL UNITED STATES, SPENDS WINTERS IN SOUTH AMERICA

ALIASES: MOSQUITO HAWK, LOCUST-EATER, BLUE SNAKE-HAWK; EASILY MISTAKEN FOR PLUMBEOUS KITE

ANGRY BEHAVIORS: DIVES ON PEOPLE AND PETS NEAR ITS NEST

HAZARD
ON THE GOLF COURSE

As anyone who's ever picked up a five-iron can tell you, golf is hard enough without having a large predatory bird zooming just a few inches from your head. Yet there's a species that's especially attracted to golf courses in the Great Plains of the United States, and over the years its angry antics have undoubtedly turned quite a few birdies into bogeys.

MADDENING MIGRANTS

Mississippi Kites like to nest in scattered trees bordering open areas, which is pretty much the definition of a golf course. In breeding season, kites become especially aggressive with young in the nest. They dive at intruders, encouraging them to leave. Kites are highly acrobatic in flight—soaring, wheeling, and swooping effortlessly. It's hard to appreciate the show, though, when you're the target. One study showed that of more than 900 "attacks" on golfers, only 3 percent involved physical contact. Nevertheless, a few kite dives have ended in bloody wounds, giving a new meaning to the word "hazard" on the course.

Watch the birdie!

Kites also breed in residential neighborhoods, and when defending nests sometimes dive on people or pets. (Kitties aren't in danger; kites mostly eat insects.) Most people, though, enjoy having Mississippi Kites around. An occasional close encounter is a small price to pay for a chance to experience this bird's beauty and grace.

Red-tailed Hawk *(Buteo jamaicensis)*

RAP SHEET

SPECIES: RED-TAILED HAWK *(BUTEO JAMAICENSIS)*

PHYSICAL DESCRIPTION: VARIED BROWNISH PLUMAGE WITH RUSTY-RED TAIL; 22 IN (56 CM) LONG WITH WINGSPAN OF 50 IN (127 CM), 2.6 LB (1.2 KG)

KNOWN WHEREABOUTS: MOST OF NORTH AND CENTRAL AMERICA

ALIASES: RED-TAIL, CHICKEN HAWK, BUZZARD

ANGRY BEHAVIORS: SLASHES WITH SHARP CLAWS

THERE WILL BE *BLOOD*

You might not call a Red-tailed Hawk chubby to its face, but that's probably what you're thinking when you see it. While most other hawks are sleek, fast flying machines, the Red-tail looks like the guy who spends too much time at the dessert table and not enough time at the gym. In fact, one scientific study showed that the average Red-tailed Hawk spends more than 90 percent of its waking hours just perching.

CAUGHT IN THE ACT

HOT-TEMPERED HAWK

It's a different story, though, when this raptor feels its nest is threatened. Every year, incidents occur in which people are injured, for unknowingly venturing too close to an active Red-tail nest. A girl taking a tour of Fenway Park in Boston was injured by a Red-tail attack in 2008 (see "Caught in the Act"). In March 2010, a woman out for a walk in Stonington, Connecticut, was clawed on her face by a nesting Red-tail, sending her to the hospital. In May 2011, a man walking on the campus of Tufts University in Somerville, Massachusetts, was struck by a Red-tail and received wounds near his eye that required 15 stitches.

These bird-human conflicts occur in part because Red-tailed Hawks, unlike some raptors, can adapt well to civilization, nesting in farmland, suburbs, and even cities. Red-tails have nested around Central Park in New York City since the early 1990s, inspiring books and television documentaries. While there have been no recorded attacks on humans in Central Park, city hawks have tried to carry off pets including a Chihuahua, a mini-dachshund, and a 15-pound cat.

A Wedge-tailed Eagle prepares to attack a hang glider.

ATTACK IN T-MINUS 5, 4, 3, 2 . . .

RAP SHEET

SPECIES: WEDGE-TAILED EAGLE (*AQUILA AUDAX*)

PHYSICAL DESCRIPTION: DARK BROWN PLUMAGE, 41 IN (104 CM) LONG WITH WINGSPAN OF 8 FT (2.4 M) OR MORE, FEMALE 12 LB (5.5 KG), MALE 8.8 LB (4 KG)

KNOWN WHEREABOUTS: AUSTRALIA AND SOUTHERN NEW GUINEA

ALIASES: WEDGIE, EAGLEHAWK

ANGRY BEHAVIORS: ATTACKS HANG GLIDERS AND PARAGLIDERS

ANTI-AIRCRAFT EAGLE

How's this for a nightmare? You're soaring more than a mile in the air in your paraglider when a pair of huge eagles attacks. They strike at your head, rip your canopy, and tangle your lines, causing you to plummet helplessly toward the ground.

NOT ONE TO SHARE THE SKY

The nightmare really happened to paraglider Nicky Moss as she was training in Australia in 2007. Her attackers were Wedge-tailed Eagles, powerful raptors with wingspans of eight feet or more. Luckily, Moss was able to regain control of her craft and landed safely. A man hang-gliding in South Australia in 1987 was not so lucky. A "Wedgie" attacked him and sent him crashing to Earth, causing serious injury. Less-serious attacks occur commonly in Australia, where Wedge-tailed Eagles dive not just on other birds but also on radio-controlled model airplanes, gliders, and even helicopters.

One of the world's largest eagles, Wedgies mate for life, and pairs defend their nesting territory against anything that seems threatening. They usually prey on rabbits, but sometimes team up to hunt animals as large as kangaroos. Thousands were shot by ranchers early in the 20th century when they were wrongly thought to be major killers of sheep.

Why so many attacks on human fliers? In part, it's simply the number of birds in the sky. Wedge-tailed Eagles are fairly abundant in Australia, much more common than most of the world's other large eagles. Lots of eagles, plus lots of radio-controlled planes and paragliders, equals lots of territorial conflicts.

Special tendons in their legs and feet keep birds from ever falling off their perches.

A Rose-breasted Grosbeak (right) aggressively defends his place on a tree limb.

An Ostrich attacks a safari guide in Tanzania.

A little traveling music, please.

RAP SHEET

SPECIES: OSTRICH *(STRUTHIO CAMELUS)*

PHYSICAL DESCRIPTION: WORLD'S LARGEST BIRD, UP TO 9 FT (2.7 M) TALL, 350 LB (160 KG); FEMALES SMALLER, 250 LB (113 KG)

KNOWN WHEREABOUTS: NATIVE TO AFRICA; INTRODUCED IN MANY OTHER AREAS

ALIASES: MBUNI (SWAHILI)

ANGRY BEHAVIORS: KICKS WITH POWERFUL LEGS AND SHARP CLAWS

BIG BIRD, BIG TROUBLE

In general, ostriches aren't particularly hostile birds. But like many species, they can get aggressive during breeding season, when males guard their harems and females defend their chicks. And when an animal stands nine feet tall and weighs more than 300 pounds, it can do serious damage even when it's just slightly annoyed.

The world's largest bird, the ostrich has immensely powerful legs and sharp claws, which it uses to kick predators or territorial intruders. And because an ostrich can run faster than 40 miles per hour, most creatures—including humans—have no chance trying to outrun one.

FARM-RAISED ANGER

Although ostrich attacks on people are rare, a few occur every year, and some result in serious injury or death. Most ostrich attacks happen not in the bird's natural range—Africans who live with ostriches know how to avoid them—but at ostrich farms (birds are raised for feathers, leather, and meat) in countries such as the United States and Australia. Handlers may get complacent around "tame" birds, or visitors may not understand that these clumps of feathers on stilts can be dangerous. (Ostriches have no respect for fame, either: The late singer Johnny Cash was once seriously injured by an ostrich he kept on his farm in Tennessee.) Ostriches may attack unsuspecting hikers who wander near farms, as happened in South Africa and Qatar in recent years.

In a world of angry birds, here's some good advice: If you have to look up to look a bird in the eye, don't make it mad.

||||||||||||||||||||||||||||||||||||||||||||||||||||||||||||||||||||||||||||||||||||||||||||||||||||||||||

YOU BETTER GIVE A HOOT 'CAUSE I'M A BRUTE.

RAP SHEET

SPECIES: TAWNY OWL (*STRIX ALUCO*)

PHYSICAL DESCRIPTION: MEDIUM-SIZE BROWNISH OWL, ABOUT 16 IN (40 CM) LONG WITH WINGSPAN OF 36 IN (91 CM), 1.2 LB (0.55 G)

KNOWN WHEREABOUTS: EUROPE AND PARTS OF ASIA AND NORTHERN AFRICA

ALIASES: HOOT OWL; EASILY MISTAKEN FOR HUME'S OWL, URAL OWL, OR BARRED OWL

ANGRY BEHAVIORS: FIERCE IN DEFENDING ITS NEST

Tawny Owl
(*Strix aluco*)

EERIE HUNTER
OF THE NIGHT

For centuries, owls have been considered omens of bad luck. Some cultures have even believed that an owl's call foretells death—as in the title of the best-selling novel *I Heard the Owl Call My Name,* based on a Native American legend.

Their large eyes and nocturnal habits, along with their eerie sounds, contribute to their mystique. But in reality, owls are simply predators—like hawks and eagles—that do their hunting at night instead of during the day, when they remain hidden and are seldom seen. It's mice, rats, and small birds that should fear this hunter.

NOCTURNAL TERROR

Like many birds, owls can be fiercely protective of their nests, and like hawks, they have sharp, powerful claws and beaks. Owls are known for aiming their attacks at the heads of people who disturb them—a scary prospect considering the weapons they possess.

The late British wildlife photographer Eric Hosking was attacked by a Tawny Owl at a nest in Wales, and lost the sight in his left eye. He had a sense of humor about the bizarre incident, though: When the time came for him to write his autobiography, he called it *An Eye for a Bird.*

A Mute Swan acts violently toward its own kind.

THAT'S FOR CALLING ME AN UGLY DUCKLING!

RAP SHEET

SPECIES: MUTE SWAN
(*CYGNUS OLOR*)

PHYSICAL DESCRIPTION: VERY LARGE WHITE WATERFOWL, 60 IN (152 CM) LONG WITH WINGSPAN OF 7.5 FT (2.3 M), 25 LB (11.5 KG)

KNOWN WHEREABOUTS: NATIVE TO EUROPE AND ASIA; INTRODUCED WORLDWIDE

ALIASES: EASILY MISTAKEN FOR WHOOPER SWAN OR TUNDRA SWAN

ANGRY BEHAVIORS: VICIOUSLY PECKS WITH BILL AND STRIKES WITH WINGS

LOOKS CAN BE DECEIVING

Everybody knows somebody who's really attractive, but whose good looks are spoiled by a bad temper. You might think of Mute Swans that way: they're the image of grace and beauty as they glide across a pond, but you'd better not get on their bad side. In an instant, that gorgeous swan can turn aggressive and violent—and a bird that big can cause real pain.

CAUGHT IN THE ACT

UGLY ATTITUDE

Mute swans are most aggressive with their own kind. Two males will fight viciously over territory, with the dominant bird sometimes pushing its victim underwater and drowning it. That anger is sometimes aimed at nonswans, including other waterfowl, dogs, and people. With its large bill, long neck, and powerful wings, a swan—the world's heaviest flying bird—can easily draw blood or seriously bruise a person, and such attacks happen often **(see "Caught in the Act")**. Kayakers and other boaters suffer the worst of swan violence, as the birds seem to view them as rivals on their watery territory. The rowing club at Cambridge, England, issued a warning in 2009 about an angry swan that had repeatedly attacked boats, capsizing one rowboat and pounding the rower with its beak.

Perhaps topping them all was a swan in Wales that over a few months in 2010 went berserk and killed 15 other swans. Local people named him Hannibal, for the serial killer in *The Silence of the Lambs*.

THEY'RE NOT CHICKEN

Seeing a Red Junglefowl for the first time, everyone has the same reaction: "Hey, that's a chicken!" And right they are. The billions of domestic chickens raised to feed people around the world are descendants of the wild Red Junglefowl, a pheasant-type bird native to the forests of southeastern Asia. Thanks to its culinary popularity, the chicken is now the most abundant species of bird on Earth.

A MATTER OF LIFE OR DEATH

While most chickens are raised for food, another type has, over the millennia, been trans-formed into one of the angriest birds in existence: the gamecock. Raised for the "sport" of cockfighting, these birds retain instincts and physical characteristics of the wild Red Jun-glefowl—particularly the males' aggressiveness toward each other. The birds fight viciously with the long spurs that naturally occur on their legs. Many fights end with the death of one combatant.

While cockfighting has been outlawed as animal cruelty in much of the world, it's still a highly popular cultural tradition in places such as Latin America, the Philippines, and Asia.

Chickens destined for the table and hens raised for egg production have been bred to be doc-ile birds, tolerant of crowded conditions. You could hardly imagine that their ancestors roam Asian jungles—or that their relatives fight for their lives in battles to the death.

Northern
Goshawk
*(Accipiter
gentilis)*

LEVEL 4 *FURIOUS*

RAP SHEET

SPECIES: NORTHERN GOSHAWK
(ACCIPITER GENTILIS)

PHYSICAL DESCRIPTION: DARK
BLUE-GRAY ABOVE, PALER
BELOW, 26 IN (66 CM) LONG,
2.8 LB (1.3 KG)

KNOWN WHEREABOUTS: MUCH
OF NORTH AMERICA, EUROPE,
AND ASIA

ALIASES: GREAT HAWK, FOREST
HAWK; EASILY MISTAKEN FOR
EURASIAN SPARROWHAWK OR
COOPER'S HAWK

ANGRY BEHAVIORS: USES POWER-
FUL TALONS TO RELENTLESSLY
ATTACK PEOPLE NEAR ITS NEST

138

THE *BADDEST* BIRD IN THE WOODS

There might be some debate about the world's angriest bird, but on the northern half of the planet, there's little doubt about the most aggressive bird in the forest: the Northern Goshawk.

OUT FOR BLOOD

The feathered equivalent of a heavily armed fighter plane, the goshawk hunts by surprising and catching prey with sheer speed and unrelenting pursuit. Its short wings and long tail give it incredible maneuverability as it weaves through tree branches or underbrush. Legendary bird artist John James Audubon observed that the goshawk "passes like a meteor through the underwood." Once it reaches its target, it strikes at a speed of more than 50 miles per hour and kills with the gripping and tearing power of its needle-sharp talons. Rabbits, squirrels, and birds up to the size of grouse and waterfowl stand little chance against a determined goshawk. As one naturalist wrote, "When its appetite for blood is once excited, the goshawk is certainly devoid of all fear."

Goshawks are extremely aggressive when they have young in the nest and don't hesitate to attack people who come near—whether unknowing passersby or scientists doing research on the species. The bird will strike over and over until the intruder leaves. One writer summed up the species as "one of the deadliest, handsomest, bravest birds of prey in the world." But the ultimate praise might be this: Attila the Hun, one of the fiercest warriors of all time, decorated his battle helmet with a figure of a goshawk.

Greater Honeyguide hatchling

HEEEEEERE'S JOHNNNNNY!

RAP SHEET

SPECIES: GREATER HONEYGUIDE (*INDICATOR INDICATOR*)

PHYSICAL DESCRIPTION: BROWN- ISH BIRD WITH CONSPICUOUS WHITE ON CHEEK (MALE) AND TAIL, ABOUT 8 IN (20 CM) LONG, 1.8 OZ (50 G)

KNOWN WHEREABOUTS: MUCH OF SUB-SAHARAN AFRICA

ALIASES: EASILY MISTAKEN FOR SCALY-THROATED HONEYGUIDE

ANGRY BEHAVIORS: CHICKS STAB AND RIP THEIR NESTMATES TO DEATH

SLAUGHTER IN THE NEST

In the savanna woodlands of sub-Saharan Africa, scientists have found what may be the most extreme example of childhood bullying in the bird world. In fact, the behavior of young Greater Honeyguides is best described as murderous.

A common bird in southern Africa, the honeyguide got its name from its habit of leading people to bees' nests. When humans break open the hive to get the honey, the honeyguide gets access to the insects and wax as food.

Honeyguides build no nests of their own. Instead, females sneak into other birds' nests to lay their eggs. Victims then raise the honeyguide chicks as their own. Young honeyguides have evolved to hatch sooner than the "real" chicks—and the Greater Honeyguide takes this parasitic relationship even further.

EVIL STEP-SIBLING

When a Greater Honeyguide emerges from the egg, its bill has sharp hooks on the tip that it uses as a deadly weapon. Having hatched before its nestmates, it promptly attacks each of them as they hatch, even though its eyes have not yet opened. The honeyguide jabs blindly, ripping the bodies of the other young birds. Far smaller than the intruder in their nest, the "real" chicks are helpless against the assault and are quickly killed. The young honeyguide then gets all the food that the parents bring to the nest. When the honeyguide is mature enough to live on its own, it leaves its foster parents. The dagger on the end of its bill, having served its purpose, has disappeared—but not the inborn aggressiveness that causes it to parasitize other birds.

||||||||||||||||||||||||||||||||||||||||||||||||||||||||||||||||||||||||||||||||||||||||||||||||||||||||||

Great
Horned
Owl (*Bubo
virginianus*)

142

Flocks of American crows routinely harass and "yell" at Great Horned Owls, who like to eat them.

Southern
Cassowary
(*Casuarius
casuarius*)

I'VE GOT A
HELMET, AND
I'M NOT AFRAID
TO USE IT

RAP SHEET

SPECIES: SOUTHERN CASSOWARY
(*CASUARIUS CASUARIUS*)

PHYSICAL DESCRIPTION: HUGE,
LONG-LEGGED BIRD WITH BLACK-
ISH BODY AND COLORFUL RED AND
BLUE BARE SKIN ON HEAD AND
NECK, ABOUT 5 FT (1.5 M) TALL,
FEMALES 120 LB (55 KG), MALES
80 LB (35 KG)

KNOWN WHEREABOUTS:
NORTHERN QUEENSLAND,
AUSTRALIA, AND NEW GUINEA

ALIASES: DOUBLE-WATTLED
CASSOWARY

ANGRY BEHAVIORS: JUMPS AND
KICKS WITH POWERFUL LEGS

YOU WON'T LIKE IT WHEN IT'S ANGRY

In a park in the seaside resort town of Cairns, Australia, there's a sign that reads, "Attention: The pounding sound of joggers' feet may aggravate cassowaries." People who live in the area understand what the sign doesn't say: ". . . and you don't want to make a cassowary angry."

Cassowaries stand more than five feet tall, with thick, powerful legs. Protective of their territories and offspring, cassowaries sometimes chase humans at speeds up to 35 miles per hour. Their most dangerous weapon is their feet: each inner toe has a long, sharp claw that can rip or puncture flesh when the bird kicks with its strong legs.

DEADLY INSTINCT

Most cassowary attacks result in minor injuries, but some can be serious. In 1926, two Australian brothers were hunting a cassowary when it came after them. One of the boys ran away, but the other was slashed in the neck and later bled to death. Many indigenous people in the rain forests of New Guinea have been injured by cassowaries, which have long been hunted for food in remote villages.

In truth, people are far more dangerous to cassowaries than vice versa. Hikers who happen to approach a cassowary are most likely to simply hear the big bird running away through the underbrush. Every now and then, though, an angry cassowary decides to chase someone along a trail, and more than one person has ended up climbing a tree to escape.

|||||||||||||||||||||||||||||||||||||||||||||||||||||||||||||||||||||||||||||||||||||||||||||||||||||||

A Northern Shrike with its impaled prey on a thorny branch

A LITTLE SNACK FOR LATER . . .

RAP SHEET

SPECIES: NORTHERN SHRIKE (*LANIUS EXCUBITOR*)

PHYSICAL DESCRIPTION: GRAY WITH BLACK WINGS AND TAIL, 10 IN (25 CM) LONG, 2.4 OZ (70 G)

KNOWN WHEREABOUTS: NORTHERN REGIONS OF NORTH AMERICA, EUROPE, AND ASIA

ALIASES: MURDERING-BIRD, NINE-KILLER, GREAT GREY SHRIKE; EASILY MISTAKEN FOR LOGGERHEAD SHRIKE, SOUTHERN GRAY SHRIKE, OR LESSER GRAY SHRIKE

ANGRY BEHAVIORS: IMPALES PREY ON THORNS FOR LATER FEASTING

BUTCHERBIRD
IMPALES ITS VICTIMS

Eww.

Pop quiz: Butcher Watchman is (A) the cruel villain in a superhero comic book, or (B) an angry bird. As you might expect from the theme of this book, the answer is B. *Lanius excubitor* ("butcher watchman") is the scientific name of the Northern Shrike—ounce for ounce among the most aggressive predators in the avian world. "Watchman" comes from an old folk belief that it keeps a lookout and calls to warn other birds of approaching danger; "butcher" refers to a habit common to shrikes around the world—a behavior as macabre as it is odd.

A TWISTED TORTURER

That's.

Shrikes prey on birds and small mammals, biting them through the neck to sever their spinal cord. After they've made a kill, they often impale the victim on a thorn or barbed wire, leaving it as an emergency food cache. A section of barbed wire may have a dozen dead mice, grasshoppers, and sparrows lined up like the meats on display in a butcher shop.

Although the Northern Shrike is smaller than a jay, it kills birds larger than itself and has been seen to attack eagles and even bears. All in all, Butcher Watchman is a tough guy you don't want to get tangled up with.

Gross.

THE ANGRIEST OF THEM ALL:
RED

Red carries the weight of leadership on his shoulders because he is the one who found the three eggs one day: He will do anything to protect them.

RED'S STORY

Red is fearless and unrelenting in his quest to protect the eggs. He sees himself as their main protector and takes full responsibility for their care. He believes that the protection of the eggs is paramount. The responsibility has forced Red to grow up very fast. Despite his young age, the rest of the birds see Red as their leader. Without him, life would be chaotic. He is eager to help anyone being harassed by the pigs.

The other Angry Birds always turn to Red in times of trouble and listen to what he has to say. Red knows that the birds are strong enough only when they stick together, and that is why he strives to keep the group united. Red respects the individuality of each of the birds in the bunch and lets them do their own thing, especially if it means they will be better equipped to guard the eggs.

But responsibility weighs heavily on Red. He doesn't fully trust the others to protect the eggs as well as he does. He often spends sleepless nights worrying about the eggs' safety and regularly checks on the birds on guard duty just to be sure they are doing their job properly. Chuck (aka Yellow Bird) is the only bird Red can confide in and express his concerns to. He wishes that Mighty Eagle would come to help the birds, and he is disappointed in Mighty's continued decision to live in complete isolation.

Continued on p. 150

WHAT MAKES HIM ANGRY

The pigs' incessant attempts to steal the eggs stress out Red. He hates the threat they pose to the eggs. Any threat to the eggs, whether from pig or bird or anything else, makes Red completely lose it. If Red feels that something is putting the eggs in danger in any way, it will feel his wrath immediately.

But it is the pigs who truly enrage Red, because they pose the biggest threat toward the eggs. They are the main reason Red had to abandon the carefree days of his youth, and he desperately misses the freedom he once took for granted. He hopes that once the eggs hatch, the pigs will no longer pose a threat to their safety and he can return to his youthful carefree days.

|||||||||||||||||||||||||||||||||||||||||||||||||||||||

RAP SHEET

NAME: RED

PHYSICAL DESCRIPTION: ROUND, RED BIRD

ALIAS: RED BIRD

HOW ANGRY IS HE: FURIOUS

WHAT MAKES HIM ANGRY: ANYTHING THAT ENDANGERS THE SAFETY OF THE EGGS. PIGS.

ANGRY BEHAVIORS: RELENTLESSLY HURLING HIMSELF AT PIGGY FORTRESSES. AGAIN AND AGAIN

HOBBIES: CHESS, PHYSICS

STRONGEST ALLY: CHUCK

LEVEL 4 *FURIOUS*

THE
WORLD'S
ANGRIEST
BIRD

DOWN-UNDER
DIVE BOMBER

You might wonder how people Down Under are brave enough to go outdoors, with all their wildlife worries—from Great White Sharks to fearsome snakes to poisonous spiders to man-eating crocodiles to deadly jellyfish. And if all that's not enough, they've got to deal with what just might be the angriest bird in the world.

Every spring, some "bad boy" Australasian Magpies become highly aggressive toward anything that gets close to their nest, swooping repeatedly at people passing by. Found over much of Australia and New Zealand, these large birds have black-and-white plumage a little like the pattern of a killer whale—hence the joking nickname "sky orca."

THE ANGRIEST OF THEM ALL

Male Australasian Magpies (no relation to the "thieving" magpies of Europe) attack walkers, joggers, horseback riders, and motorcyclists, but they especially dislike bicyclists. A magpie may follow a biker for a hundred yards or more, diving over and over and occasionally striking the head or back. While most magpie attacks are only annoying, some are no joke at all.

Serious stab wounds sometimes result from jabs of the magpie's sharp beak. Bicyclists have been knocked off their bikes, and riders have been thrown from spooked horses. In 2010, a

Continued on p. 154

12-year-old boy on a bicycle was killed in traffic while fleeing an aerial attack. Many postal workers in Australia ride bicycles on their routes, and magpies have been known to learn the exact time they appear, standing guard for a daily attack.

Suggestions abound for defending against magpie encounters. Wildlife departments offer online graphics of huge eyes that people can print and attach to the back of their hats. Some bicyclists say that hanging shiny tinsel from a helmet scares magpies away. People without helmets are advised to wear a cardboard box or a plastic ice-cream carton on their heads—but you have to think that walking around wearing a box might be even less appealing than a magpie peck.

THE BOYS' CLUB

A survey in Australia revealed that more than 90 percent of men and 72 percent of women had been attacked by a magpie at some point in their lives. (Australasian Magpies seem to especially resent male humans. Men made up two-thirds of all hospital emergency visits caused by magpie attacks.) Luckily, the season for magpie anger is relatively short: just six weeks or so during the spring when the birds have young in the nest.

In fact, only a small percentage of magpies attack people. But because the species so commonly nests in cities and suburbs, the total number of bird-people incidents runs into the thousands each year. And that adds up to what's probably the world champion angry bird.

An Australasian
Magpie attacks
a bicyclist.

SPECIES: AUSTRALASIAN MAGPIE (*GYMNORHINA TIBICEN*)

PHYSICAL DESCRIPTION: LARGE BLACK-AND-WHITE SONGBIRD, 16 IN (40 CM) LONG, 12 OZ (350 G)

KNOWN WHEREABOUTS: AUSTRALIA AND PARTS OF NEW GUINEA; INTRODUCED INTO NEW ZEALAND

ALIASES: PIPING CROW, SKY ORCA

ANGRY BEHAVIORS: SWOOPING AT AND JABBING PEOPLE NEAR ITS NEST

Look out behind you!

Angry Birds in Scientific Order

Family Struthionidae
Ostrich (*Struthio camelus*) 130

Family Casuariidae
Southern Cassowary (*Casuarius casuarius*) 144

Family Dromaiidae
Emu (*Dromaius novaehollandiae*) 56

Family Anatidae
Egyptian Goose (*Alopochen aegyptiaca*) 80
Canada Goose (*Branta canadensis*) 92
Mute Swan (*Cygnus olor*) 134

Family Numididae
Helmeted Guineafowl (*Numida meleagris*) 12

Family Phasianidae
Red Junglefowl (*Gallus gallus*) 136
Eurasian Capercaillie (*Tetrao urogallus*) 106
Wild Turkey (*Meleagris gallopavo*) 98

Family Spheniscidae
Adélie Penguin (*Pygoscelis adeliae*) 16

Family Procellariidae
Northern Fulmar (*Fulmarus glacialis*) 118

Family Fregatidae
Magnificent Frigatebird (*Fregata magnificens*) 42

Family Sulidae
Northern Gannet (*Morus bassanus*) 54
Nazca Booby (*Sula granti*) 102

Family Pelecanidae
Great White Pelican (*Pelecanus onocrotalus*) 22

Family Accipitridae
Mississippi Kite (*Ictinia mississippiensis*) 122
Lappet-faced Vulture (*Torgos tracheliotus*) 116
Northern Goshawk (*Accipiter gentilis*) 138
Red-tailed Hawk (*Buteo jamaicensis*) 124
Harpy Eagle (*Harpia harpyja*) 110
Wedge-tailed Eagle (*Aquila audax*) 126

Family Falconidae
Striated Caracara (*Phalcoboenus australis*) 62

Family Rallidae
Eurasian Coot (*Fulica atra*) 82

Family Cariamidae
Red-legged Seriema (*Cariama cristata*) 72

Family Charadriidae
Masked Lapwing (*Vanellus miles*) 76

Family Scolopacidae
Ruff (*Philomachus pugnax*) 52

Family Laridae
Herring Gull (*Larus argentatus*) 100

Family Stercorariidae
Parasitic jaeger (*Stercorarius parasiticus*) 114

Family Strigopidae
Kea (*Nestor notabilis*) 88

Family Strigidae
Tawny Owl (*Strix aluco*) 132

Family Trochilidae
Rufous Hummingbird (*Selasphorus rufus*) 14

Family Ramphastidae
Toco Toucan (*Ramphastos toco*) 32

Family Indicatoridae
Greater Honeyguide *(Indicator indicator)* 140

Family Tyrannidae
Eastern Kingbird *(Tyrannus tyrannus)* 46
Great Kiskadee *(Pitangus sulphuratus)* 70

Family Meliphagidae
Tui *(Prosthemadera novaeseelandiae)* 44
Noisy Miner *(Manorina melanocephala)* 90

Family Cracticidae
Australasian Magpie *(Gymnorhina tibicen)* 155

Family Pachycephalidae
Crested Bellbird *(Oreoica gutturalis)* 36

Family Laniidae
Northern Shrike *(Lanius excubitor)* 146

Family Corvidae
Blue Jay *(Cyanocitta cristata)* 108
Eurasian Magpie *(Pica pica)* 26
Common Raven *(Corvus corax)* 60

Family Troglodytidae
House Wren *(Troglodytes aedon)* 18

Family Turdidae
Fieldfare *(Turdus pilaris)* 28

Family Mimidae
Northern Mockingbird *(Mimus polyglottos)* 64

Family Sturnidae
European Starling *(Sturnus vulgaris)* 66

Family Parulidae
Yellow Warbler *(Setophaga petechia)* 24

Family Cardinalidae
Northern Cardinal *(Cardinalis cardinalis)* 34

Acknowledgments

We would like to extend our thanks to the terrific team who worked so hard to make this project come together so quickly and so well.

Rovio

Sanna Lukander, Antti Grönlund, Hanna Silvennoinen, Jan Schulte-Tigges, Jaakko Sarno, Olga Budanova, Sini Matikainen, and Mari Elomäki

National Geographic

Amy Briggs, Bridget A. English, Jonathan Halling, Stewart Bean, Matt Propert, Galen Young, Judith Klein, Anna Zusman, Lisa A. Walker, Dee Wong, and Jonathan Alderfer

Illustration Credits

Front cover, © Art Wolfe/www.artwolfe.com; back cover, Raymond Barlow/National Geographic My Shot; 2, courtesy of Wikipedia (http://en.wikipedia.org/wiki/File:Birdsniper.jpg); 8-9, Duncan Usher/National Geographic Stock; 12, Bill Coster/NHPA/Photoshot; 14, Oxford Scientific/Getty; 16, Ted Mead/Getty; 17, Ralph Lee Hopkins/National Geographic Stock; 18, Michael Woodruff/Shutterstock; 20-21, Joe Petersburger/National Geographic Stock; 22, Craig Shepheard/Corbis/Demotix; 23, Nine/Universal News and Sport; 24, Steve Byland/Shutterstock; 25, Earl Reinink; 26, Asturianu/Shutterstock; 28, Mike Lane/Alamy; 30, Don Klein/Superstock; 32, Jason Idzerda; 34, Steve Happ; 36-37, Seth Resnick/Getty/Science Faction; 38, Frans Lanting/Corbis; 40-41, Richard Berry/Design Pics Inc./Alamy; 42, Richard Spranger; 44, Catherine Miller; 48-49, VGramitikov/Shutterstock; 52, Ocean/Corbis; 54, Norbert Rosing/National Geographic Stock; 56, Josly Almeida/National Geographic Stock; 58-59, Efren Ricalde/National Geographic My Shot; 60, Proehl Proehl/Getty/Picture Press; 62, John Shaw/Getty; 63, courtesy of National Geographic Digital Motion; 64, Cliff Collings; 65, Lou Guillette; 66, Alfred & Fabiola Forns/Solent; 68, Sue Flood/Getty; 70, Pete Oxford/National Geographic Stock; 72-73, Arthur Morris/Corbis; 74, Joos Schoeman/Alamy; 75, Arnon Azmon; 78-79, Nic Bothma/Corbis; 80, M. Frankling/Getty/Flickr RF; 84-85, Patricia Fitzgerald/National Geographic My Shot; 88, John Cancalosi/Alamy; 90, Gerry Pearce/Alamy; 92, Jon Vermilye; 93, Associated Press/Douglas Tesner; 94-95, Tui De Roy/National Geographic Stock; 96, Boston Globe/Getty; 97, Emily Anne Epstein/Corbis; 98-99, Brian Norcross/Alamy; 100, Paul Kingston/North News; 102, David Thyberg; 104, Jari Peltomaki; 105, courtesy of Wikipedia (http://fi.wikipedia.org/wiki/Tiedosto:Capercaillie%282%29.JPG); 106, Jim Brandenburg/Minden Pictures; 108, Kevin Schafer/Corbis; 110-111, Keith Ringland/Getty; 112, Andrew Parkinson/Nature Picture Library; 114, Anup Shah/Getty; 116, Jouan Ruis/Nature Picture Library; 120-121, Jason Hosking/Getty; 122, David Seibel; 124, Marcus Armani/National Geographic My Shot; 125, Boston Globe/Getty; 126, Kathryn O'Riordan; 128-129, Gerald Marella/Shutterstock; 130, Gert-Jan Seisling; 132, Mark Bridger/Shutterstock; 134, Ronald Wittek/Getty; 135, Michael S. Gordon/The Republican; 136, Tier Und Naturfotografie J & C Sohns/Getty; 138, Fred Hazelhoff/Getty/Minden Pictures; 140, Claire Spottiswoode; 142-143, Patricia Fitzgerald/National Geographic My Shot; 144, Mark Cawardine/Getty; 146, Juniors Bildarchiv/Alamy; 152, Michael Davidson; 154-155, Mark Calleja/Newspix.

ROCKET FUEL FOR YOUR BRAIN

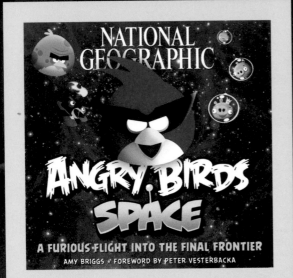

When it comes to ANGRY BIRDS, a little understanding can go a long way! So don't launch into space without the official companion book to the Angry Birds Space game, which follows the furious fliers on their quest to explore the galaxy, defeat the pigs, and rescue their precious eggs. Filled with incredible illustrations and awesome facts, it's just the edge you need to better understand the planets, moons, stars, and mysteries of the universe...and to navigate the galaxy and beyond.

A FUN GUIDE AND GREAT GIFT FOR ANGRY BIRDS ADDICTS EVERYWHERE

AVAILABLE WHEREVER BOOKS ARE SOLD

and at shopng.com/AngryBirds

FIND ALL ANGRY BIRDS GAMES AT ANGRYBIRDS.COM

NATIONAL
GEOGRAPHIC   Facebook.com/NatGeoBooks